quick quick slow

A NEW TAKE ON SLOW-COOKED RECIPES COMBINED WITH FUN & EASY QUICK ONES

allegra mcevedy
with *Deniz Safa*

PHOTOGRAPHY BY GEORGIA GLYNN SMITH

K KYLE BOOKS

allegra mcevedy
with Deniz Safa

quick quick slow

A NEW TAKE ON SLOW-COOKED RECIPES COMBINED WITH FUN & EASY QUICK ONES

First published in Great Britain in 2016 by
Kyle Books, an imprint of Kyle Cathie Ltd
192–198 Vauxhall Bridge Road
London SW1V 1DX
general.enquiries@kylebooks.com
www.kylebooks.co.uk

10 9 8 7 6 5 4 3 2 1

ISBN 978 0 85783 360 0

Project Editor: Tara O'Sullivan
Editorial Assistant: Amberley Lowis
Art Director and Designer: Anita Mangan
Design Assistant: Ewa Lefmann
Photographer: Georgia Glynn Smith
Illustrator: Anita Mangan
Food Stylist: Allegra McEvedy
Prop Stylist: Emily Ezekiel
Production: Nic Jones and Gemma John

A Cataloguing in Publication record for this title is
available from the British Library.

Colour reproduction by F1 Colour
Printed and bound in China by 1010 International
Printing Ltd

FOR *isabelle* AND *jiggy*

contents

introduction

It was the hot summer of 2014, and I was sitting at a table for two in Exmouth market outside my now extinguished piggy restaurant, Blackfoot. My past publisher and long-time friend Kyle (she of the 'K' on the spine of this book) was opposite me, and as we basked in the afternoon sunshine she rather got on one, telling me after a glass or two that really what I should do is stop writing hefty books that appealed to rather a select audience (and in truth were – for me at least – borne out of the landmark events in my life. i.e. dead mum; dead dad; daughter born, to sum it up crudely) and write something that was a simpler concept, less traumatic for me and more saleable.

'Why don't you write a book about slow-cooking?' she said. 'It's the kind of food people know you for: accessible, cheap, yummy home cooking.'

Even through the haze of the heat and the bottom of the Brouilly, I could see that it wasn't a stupid idea, but I was in a bit of a busy time so I just let it mull and ferment in my subconscious till life calmed down a bit.

But as it slowly bubbled away in there, I became increasingly aware of a niggling low-lying issue: I really did like the idea of slow-cooking, however the thought of writing a whole book on it failed to ignite one iota of enthusiasm... never a good way to enter a project, let alone one as epic as writing a book. And can you imagine the recipe testing? I've only got two ovens, so you stick a pot in each one, walk away, come back in however many hours... where's the fun in that? And with an average of 120 recipes a book, think about how long that would take? I began to realise that a book on just slow cooking might not be right for me.

Enter the foxtrot.

'Slow Quick Quick,' said Len, explaining the dance from the background of our sitting room (as in on the telly, just incase you think I hang with Len).

It was an instant epiphany: now *that* was a book I wanted to write. The recipes would come in threes, one Slow and two (mostly standalone) bolt-on Quicks to make it a meal/finish the job/crowning touches/give you some fun direction with leftovers.

A variety of tempos, more pace, and a perfect joining of the old world cooking that's enjoying such a renaissance these last couple of decades with contemporary needs.

Elizabeth D smashed with Jamie's 15-minute meals. Could it get any better – or any more useful – for our times??

Excitedly I ran it past my trusted agent (and great buddy) Rosemary, who liked the twist on the original plan. Although Kyle was initially less sure, she could see that really that was the book I wanted to write, and I'm grateful to her for letting me.

In one last turn of the knife to really see off the slow-cooking book (that I'd even got as far as giving a title to: 'Low & Slow'. Yawn) I decided that the Slow in my foxtrot wasn't just going to be about bunging it in the oven and walking away... no, it was going to be a whole lot more esoteric, poetic and yes, less simple than that: my slows were about a waving of the wand and a passing of time. That opened up wonderful worlds of pickling, marinating, proving, infusing, preserving, pressing, curing and even some super-chilled-out sitting and resting. As well as, of course, a decent show of long-term oven residents, as a nod to Kyle's original idea.

So given that I'd blown the brief completely, I then made myself a new set of rules: whatever happened to the Slows, it had to take more than two hours and less than a month; the key being that as mealtime approached, you knew you had already taken care of a big chunk of the work. Having said that, if you're more inclined to Jamie than Elizabeth, some of my more eccentric Slows are utterly circumnavigable, like making bread or preserved lemons... and I'll just leave that one with you.

Similarly, I self-stipulated that the Quicks had to be 20 minutes or under... though we all know what rules are there for (and *you* try to make the rosti on page 107 from start to finish in 20 minutes!). So having carefully and usefully set these rules up, I then broke them more times than I can hold in my head, so maybe it's fairer to call them guidelines.

As I signed the contract back in the summer of 2015 I had a lingering worry that I was going to feel less affectionate about this book, than the aforementioned ones that centered around my family. But hand on heart I can say that I think these are some of the best recipes I've ever come up with...and had the most fun doing. Because we all know that you can't really do your best work if you're not happy – the synapses just don't fire in the same electric way - and for me a fair amount of

happy means a bit of silly, and boy did we laugh as we cooked (and by 'we', I mean my co-cook on this project, the awesome, talented Deniz Safa). And out of our mirth rose a plethora of Slows, which is where we started each merry threesome. A ridiculously tingly 2-day Szechuan pork belly; some punchy Vietnamese overnight pickles; whiskey salmon that likes a two day marinade in the good stuff; 7-hour leg of lamb with 70 cloves of garlic; crusty Belgian beer bread, and a sticky, rum-soaked gingerbread that sits, getting gooier, for a week... to name but a few.

And then *more* creative free-thinking as we came up with their accompanying Quicks, so that our gingerbread became a twist on my favourite cocktail, Dark & Stormy, with a homemade lime butter (as in you make the butter from cream in 10 mins) and Angostura honeycomb. Our Belgian beer bread was of course always going to have quick-cook mussels alongside, to dunk it in, but it's almost the vite frites that steal the show. The heavily spiced, deep flavours of the pork belly got partnered up with a cooling pecan coleslaw...not to mention the outrageous Scooby Sarnie that I couldn't resist the next day. The clean flavours of our Asian pickles found a home with some serene steamed scallops backed up by blackened garlic broccolini and a third quick in tomorrow's almost instant bahn mi. And having gorged on the 7:70 leg of lamb, it miraculously turns into Moroccan spiced Freekeh to give a Levant leaning to another day's meal.

Even across this small snapshot of what lies ahead, there are simple suppers, light lunches, family feasts, more stylish dishes for when folks are over, fun ones for kids to eat and cook, party snacks and even leftovers for the next day.

And although they may not all sound like the simplest of cooks, the greatest part of all is that as the countdown to mealtime draws closer, the majority of the work is already done – the flavours at the heart of your meal are secured, in the bag, and all that's left to pull together is a Quick or two to support, enhance and round off the main shebang. Nifty!

NOTES AND ASSUMPTIONS:

- All eggs should be free-range and medium sized (apparently it hurts them to push out the large ones... just like us).

- All pepper mentioned is black (I'm a bit funny about white).

- All butter is salted unless specified unsalted.

- If you use shop-bought stock, go with little tubettes of concentrate rather than cubes.

KEY: SLOW RECIPE   QUICK RECIPE

[signature]

May 2016

chapter one
chicken & other birds

This is a bonus chapter: there are 25% more recipes in it for FREE, because hey, who doesn't like chicken? What we have here are a couple of takes on the whole bird – one for the hob, one in the oven – some party wings, a slightly needy but fabulous duck curry, two turkeys (some epically fun drummers and a slightly more sane burger recipe)... and a partridge (no pear tree required). From their origins in Asia, our feathered friends have clucked their way all over the planet, and the recipes that follow reflect that, from Thailand to Turkey to Tennessee (well maybe not exactly Tennessee, but somewhere in the Southern States).

Unless it's Christmas and you're going for a Big Roast Bird, poultry doesn't really lend itself to slow cooking without some wetness to work with – there's nothing in the world worse than dry breasts – so our whole birds are either pot-braised or poached (except the little guy who gets a hard-and-fast roast, thus just squeezing in under the line as a 'Quick'), or I've gone with component parts, like wings and drummers... and in one case opted for the smallest version of any animal possible, that is to say, minced. Because small really can be beautiful, and in the case of our Turkish Turkey Burgers – aka 'The McTurco'– it really is.

POT-BRAISED CHICKEN

PREP: 30 MINS • COOK: 2 HOURS 20 MINS

PEA & PARSLEY DUMPLINGS

PREP: 10 MINS • COOK: 20 MINS

CHICKEN & CHICORY SALAD
WITH BURNT PHIL'S DRESSING

PREP: 10 MINS

Slow-cooked Chook

This is a two for today and one for tomorrow situation; as eats they couldn't be more different, but to me they both have an air of yesteryear. The first meal is one of comfort and familiarity, old-school English food done well... and by that I mean with dumplings (pea and parsley, as all the best British meals involve peas). And whilst the next day's salad is suitably contrasting to the pot-braise it's (mostly) built of centuries-old native ingredients, so in spirit at least wouldn't feel out of place in an eighteenth century English cookbook.

As it stands, this makes a brace of meals for two; to turn the slow-cooked chook into a meal for four, simply buy a larger bird (like 1.5+kg) and double the dumpling recipe... but just as a heads-up your adventure will probably end there as I don't reckon there'll be enough chicken left to make the salad.

And in case you were wondering, the dressing that really is the making of the salad is so named because on the day my great chef friend Phil came round my house and made it, he'd just lost half the skin on his thigh after an altercation in a crazy Sunday lunch service with a tray of bazillion-degree Yorkies. Still turned up for work the next day though, like a true Yorkshireman.

POT-BRAISED CHICKEN

SERVES 2

Timeline

3 HOURS BEFORE
Get chicken working

ANYTIME WHILE THE BIRD IS COOKING
Make the dumplings

WHEN CHOOK COOKED
Drop in dumplings

NEXT DAY
Make chicken and chicory salad

1 healthy tablespoon olive oil

1 chicken (about 1.2–1.5kg), preferably corn-fed

3 cloves of garlic, sliced

120ml (small glass) white wine

2 tablespoons sherry vinegar

30g butter

5–6 medium-sized waxy potatoes (like Rattes), washed

1 large carrot, scrubbed and sliced into 4

4 banana shallots, peeled and left whole

2 bay leaves

10ish stalks of thyme, tied together with string

1 litre chicken stock

S & P

○ Preheat the oven to 150°C/130°C fan/gas mark 2 and get your hands on an ovenproof pot/pan (you know, like a Le Creuset) that's big enough to hold all the ingredients.

○ Whack it on a high heat, pour in the oil and as it gets searingly hot, take the time to season your chicken all over.

○ Lay the chicken in the hot oil, breast-side down, then once they're good and dark golden, use tongs to do the same on all its aspects: both the leg sides, one after the other, then stand it on end – wishbone-down – and finally breasts up. Once she's good and tanned, lift out and put to one side.

○ Chuck in the garlic and cook until golden, which won't take long, so be ready with wine in hand (always). Whilst the wine is reducing, add the sherry vinegar and butter, then reduce the heat and lay the chicken back in there, breast-side up.

○ Pack the spuds, veg and herbs in and around the chicken (I stuff the cavity of the bird with whole shallots), then pour in the stock around the edges, not over the chook. The liquid should cover the veg and top of the legs (it doesn't matter if the crown is sticking out), so top up with hot water if needed.

○ Season the veg, then put a lid on and stick it in the oven for 2 hours, by which point it'll be ready for dumplings (see below).

○ When the dumplings are done, lift the chicken out for ease of carving and serve up in warmed shallow bowls, with the dumplings, braising veg and a couple of ladles of stock.

Fill your boots – there should still be enough for tomorrow's salad, as it's amazing how much meat can be scrounged from a pretty spent-looking carcass.

PEA & PARSLEY DUMPLINGS

SERVES 2
(MAKES 6 = 3 EACH)

50g plain flour, plus extra for dusting

¼ teaspoon baking powder

50g frozen peas, defrosted and crushed with the side of a knife

1–2 spring onions, sliced

25g shredded suet

a handful (10g) of flat-leaf parsley, finely chopped

heaped ¼ teaspoon salt and a good showing of black pepper

○ Put everything in a mixing bowl, give it a brief stir, then pour in about 3 tablespoons of cold water to bring it together.

○ Split the dough in half and with lightly floured hands roll three dumplings from each one. (If they're not needed for a while, keep under a tea towel on the side.)

○ When the chook has had its 2 hours in the oven, carefully lift the pot out and take off the lid. Plop the dumplings into the stock, making sure that they are at least three-quarters submerged, then slip the lid on again and put back in the oven for 20 minutes.

CHICKEN & CHICORY SALAD
WITH BURNT PHIL'S CITRUS DRESSING

FOR 2 (OR 1 INSANELY STARVACEOUS BOD)

30g hazelnuts, skinned and whole

150–200g cooked chicken, picked from yesterday's carcass

2 bulbs chicory, cut into leaves

2 vine-ripened tomatoes, chunkily diced, or a handful of cherries, halved

a handful (40g-ish) of sugar snap peas, sliced on the oblique

2 spring onions, sliced

BURNT PHIL'S CITRUS DRESSING*

zest and juice of 1 lemon

zest and juice of 1 lime

1 heaped teaspoon wholegrain mustard

1 tablespoon golden syrup (or honey as a back-up)

3 tablespoons extra virgin olive oil

FOR THE CROUTONS

2 thick slices (80g) white bread, crusts off and cut into 3cm-ish dice (sourdough works well but use whatever's dying in the bread bin)

good splash of olive oil

1 clove of garlic, chopped

S & P

* Makes about twice what you need but a good dressing is always handy to have around.

○ Preheat the oven to 200°C/180°C fan/gas mark 6. As the oven's coming up to speed, knock up the dressing as it does well to sit for a few minutes: just put everything in a jam jar and give it a good shake.

○ For the croutons, toss the bread chunks with the olive oil, garlic and some salt and pepper. Spread out onto a baking tray so they're not all piled up, then scatter the hazelnuts in and around them and stick in the oven.

○ After 5ish minutes, the croutons should be starting to brown, so give them a shuffle-turn, then push them and the nuts up to one end of the tray and spread the chicken out at the other end to warm through. Put back in the oven for 5–7 minutes until the croutons are golden brown and the nuts are nicely toasted.

○ Load your chosen salad bowl up with the chicory, tomatoes, sugar snaps, spring onions and, once ready, tip the hot stuff in there too.

○ Give the dressing a good shake, then pour about half of it in. Taste, season and away you go.

party
snarfes

party snarfes

WINGS OF FIRE

PREP: 5 MINS • LEAVE: OVERNIGHT • COOK: 30 MINS

PIREAUS PIZZAS

PREP: 5 MINS • COOK: 5 MINS

WIN-WIN DOLCELATTE DIP

PREP: 5 MINS

AS A TRIUMVIRATE, THESE SHOULD SATISFY 8ISH FOLKS

It's only recipe collective no. 2, and we've already got a different take on our Quick Quick Slow set up: not a mains with sides, nor a couple of dishes for today with a carry over to tomorrow, but more for a party scenario – ideal for anything from nibbles with drinks to a footie feast.

The wings themselves are pretty ferocious as they are, which is why it works so well for them to be tempered by the cooling, creamy dip.

About that dip: it's a winner every time and seemingly indestructible – by virtue of its simple scrumminess it appears not just here but with the spectacular Party Piece Baked Butternut on page 164. As a result of having to do a fair amount of retesting on both the wings to get their heat level right, and the butternut, which turned out ace but started out a bit weird, this simple bung-in-and-blitz party pleaser turned out to be the most tested recipe in the book.

Depending on how much of an allium-phile you are – big fan over here – you may want to know that the onionyness just keeps getting better and bigger over days. In fact, I found that this baby lasts so long in the fridge that I began to get freaked out and ended up throwing away the last tiny bit: even if the principal ingredient is based on mould, there's something wrong with it still tasting that good a week later.

And then to contrast with the roar of the wings and the sharp, richness of my NASA-worthy dip, in strolls the Piraeus Pizza – all the principles of pizza (as in bready base, tomato and cheese), but put together in a decidedly fresher, more Greekish way.

WINGS OF FIRE

MAKES 15–25 PIECES (DEPENDING ON IF YOU GOT THEM FROM A BUTCHER OR SUPERMARKET)

2kg chicken wings

2 cloves of garlic, chopped

2 tablespoons runny honey

4 tablespoons English mustard

300ml red wine vinegar

4 tablespoons soft dark brown sugar

½ teaspoon smoked paprika

1 teaspoon Chinese five-spice

2 teaspoons Tabasco

2 teaspoons chilli flakes

300g tomato ketchup

plus 1–2 red chillies, sliced, to finish

S & P

○ Bring out your biggest bowl/bucket and put absolutely everything except the sliced chillies in there. Be sure to give the wings a good roll around to coat well, then cover with clingfilm (or if fridge space runs at a premium in your house, too, then tip into a bin bag) and leave in the fridge overnight.

○ When you're 45 minutes away from wanting wings, preheat the oven to 240°C/220°C fan/gas mark 9 and line two big baking trays with greaseproof paper.

○ Spread the wings out on the baking trays, rounded-side up, and cook the hell out of them, one tray at a time, for about 30–35 minutes on the top shelf until the meat next to the bone comes away cleanly.

Scatter with sliced chillies at the end: go hard or go home.

PIREAUS PIZZAS

FOR THE TOPPING

250g packet halloumi, grated on
the big holes

1 clove of garlic, minced

1 teaspoon dried oregano

150g cherry tomatoes, cut into
quarters

S & P

TO SERVE

3 khobez flatbreads
(20cm diameter)

extra virgin olive oil, for drizzling

squeeze of lemon, to finish

big handful of mint leaves, washed
and chopped

○ Preheat your grill to medium–high. Mix
together all the topping ingredients in a bowl,
then season and divide loosely into three.

○ Spread one-third of the mix onto each
flatbread: in contrast to its Italian namesake
take the filling right to the edges, then drizzle
all over with olive oil.

○ Pop them under the grill one or two at a time –
but don't go far, as depending on the strength
of your grill, it can all happen pretty quickly.
They're ready when the cheese has started to
melt and the bread is crisp around the edges.

○ Squeeze well with lemon, scatter on the mint,
cut each pizza into six wedges and get your
party started.

Timeline

DAY/NIGHT BEFORE
Marinate wings

ANYTIME ON THE DAY
Knock up dip

**45 MINUTES BEFORE
PARTY TIME**
Preheat oven
Cook wings
Cut crudités
Build and grill pizzas

WIN-WIN
DOLCELATTE DIP

**MAKES A HAPPY AMOUNT FOR
SCOOPING UP WITH THE VEG AND WINGS**

300g cheap Dolcelatte

3 spring onions, thinly sliced

120g mayonnaise

70g crème fraîche

1½ tablespoons lemon juice

a little bit of salt and plenty of
freshly ground black pepper

VEG TO SERVE

sticks of celery/cucumber/carrot

whole roast baby beetroot

radishes

(or whatever you fancy)

○ Put 50g of the cheese and the spring onions
aside, then blitz everything else in a food
processor until smooth and creamy.

○ Use a spatula to scrape into a bowl, then
squish the last of the cheese in to give
it texture.

○ Finish with the spring onions, stirring most
in but saving a few for the top, along with a
crack or two of black pepper.

○ Everyone's a winner, baby.

soul-feeding food (poach, puff & pot)

SIMPLE POACHED CHICKEN

PREP: 5 MINS • COOK: 2-3 HOURS

NIGHT-TIME PUFFS

PREP: 20ISH MINS • COOK: 20 MINS

GET BETTER SOUP

PREP: 5 MINS • COOK: 10 MINS

This trio is like a three-armed cuddle: by the time you've had your fill you'll be relaxed, loved-up and have a wellbeing rating that blows the kombucha 'n' kale crowd out of the ballpark.

First we make our simple stock, and then we lie in it. No, and then we make some fine turnovers and a soup that is designed for living (as opposed to dying, which is how you can feel when you're a bit down or suffering from flu or a cold).

Our slow is at the start and the heart of it: just a simple poached chicken, yielding both a great stock (the backbone of our soup) and the cooked chix and veg that are our pastry filling-to-be. The puffs go down a treat with kiddies, but if they are your chosen destination, my advice is to leave out/tone down the mustard.

There is a bit of crossover with these three as some of the stock goes to bind our filling, and a leg of the chicken is nicked for the soup. But really they are all one big happy family, so there's no nicking, just sharing...

SIMPLE POACHED CHICKEN

MAKES 1 COOKED CHOOK, PLUS ABOUT A LITRE OF STOCK...
JUST WHAT YOU NEED FOR THE REST OF THIS HAPPY THREESOME

1 smallish chicken (about 1.2kg)

couple of sprigs of rosemary

handful of thyme stalks, tied with string to the rosemary

3 bay leaves

2 carrots (250g), peeled and left whole

1 leek, roots trimmed, halved lengthways, but still held together at the base (make sure it's well washed too; leeks can be right dirty buggers)

1 bulb of garlic, left whole

○ Put the chicken in a pot big enough to be able to put the lid on without squiffing and pour on enough cold water to pretty much cover – you don't need to fill it right to the top as inevitably that'll make a mess of your hob at some point in the next couple of hours, and it doesn't matter if the top of the breasts is sticking out.

○ Toss the herbs in there, put the lid on, bring to the boil, give it a good skim, then reduce the heat to the lowest setting so it's just steaming – no bubbles and no lid.

○ After an hour, add the veg and garlic and turn the heat up again so it's simmering away nicely – the aim here is to reduce and strengthen the stock as the veg cooks.

○ Give it another 30 minutes, then lift the chicken and veg out, leaving the garlic and herbs in there. Put the chicken somewhere to cool as you want to get picking it soon.

○ Turn the heat up and keep reducing the stock until it's down to about a litre (this takes anywhere from 30–50 minutes depending on the size of your pan) and has a decent strength of flavour, at which point strain it through a sieve and chuck away the garlic, herbs and scrot.

○ Pour/ladle a rough third into a bowl/mug/whatevs for the puff recipe and the remainder goes soup-wards.

MAKES 6 PUFFS WITH ENOUGH CHICKEN LEFTOVER FOR THE GET BETTER SOUP. IF YOU WANT FEWER PUFFS AND MORE SOUP (THE BETTER FREEZING OPTION FOR FORWARD PLANNERS), KNOCK BACK THE WEIGHTS BELOW AND MAKE A BONZO BUMPER BOOSTER ZUPPA!

NIGHT-TIME PUFFS

the poached chicken (minus a
    leg for the Get Better Soup on
    page 20), plus the leek and one
    of the carrots

50g butter

60g plain flour, plus extra for
    dusting

⅓ (300ml-ish) of the reduced
    chicken stock

1 tablespoon wholegrain mustard

1 tablespoon Dijon mustard

2 x 320g packets pre-rolled puff
    pastry

1 egg, beaten with 2 tablespoons
    milk

S & P

○ First pick the chix, discarding all the skin and bones, and don't forget to turn it over and whip the oysters out too (which frankly I think you should just pop in your mouth right now... you deserve it).

○ Roughly chop the pile of meat along with the cooked leek and carrot.

○ Gently melt the butter in a saucepan big enough to hold all the ingredients (except the pastry, numbat) and add the flour to make a roux. Stir occasionally with a wooden spoon for a good few minutes, then change your tool to a whisk and pour in a rough third of the measured stock.

○ Turn the heat up to medium as you whisk to a smooth paste, then add the next third, whisk till smooth again and repeat with the last lot.

○ Back to the wooden spoon: stir in the chicken, veg and both mustards, then season well to taste.

○ Spread out on a tray to cool as it needs to be room temp or colder when you load it into the pastry. Window sill/doorstep is my top tip.

○ Preheat the oven to 220°C/200°C fan/gas mark 7. Lightly dust your work surface with flour and lay down the pre-rolled pastry sheets. Find something round with a 16–18cm diameter (like a side plate), cut out two circles from each sheet, then roll out the off-cuts to make the last two. Finally, lightly roll each circle to make them oval.

○ Once the chix mix has cooled, roughly divide it into six. Spoon a pile into the middle of the top half of each oval, leaving enough space around the edge for the pastry to seal.

○ Brush all around the pile with eggwash, then fold the bottom half over, pressing it right up against the base of the chix so you get a decent dome. Lightly push down all around with your fingertips, then trim off any excess pastry and seal with the tines of a fork. Prick each one three times on top to let the steam out as it cooks.

○ Lift them onto two lightly oiled/buttered baking trays, three on each, and egg-wash all over the outsides.

○ There's an option here to make little pastry pretties with the off-cuts and stick them on, but then this recipe would become even less of a Quick... but if you do, don't forget to egg-wash them too.

○ Bake on the top and middle shelves of the oven for 15–20 minutes, swapping them round halfway through, until shiny and golden and Gregg would be proud of you.

GET BETTER SOUP

FROM THE STOCK PAN

1 cooked chicken leg

²/₃ (about 600–700ml) of the reduced chicken stock

1 carrot, roughly diced

TO FINISH

2 cloves of garlic, roughly chopped

50g pasta

3 heaped tablespoons Greek yogurt

a good handful baby spinach, roughly chopped

S & P

○ Peel the skin from the chicken leg and throw it (unless you like boiled chicken skin, in which case nosh it now). Pick the meat from the bones and roughly shred.

○ Put the stock, cooked chicken, carrot, garlic and pasta into a pan on a medium heat. Once it's steaming, taste for seasoning (assuming, of course, you still have a sense of taste) – both the stock and the pasta will take a fair amount of salt to get the most out of them.

○ Whilst the pasta is cooking, measure the yogurt into a little bowl. Once the pasta's ready, pour a ladleful of the hot stock onto the yogurt and mix together with a fork. Now whisk this back into the remainder of the soup – doing it this way stops the yogurt from curdling.

○ Have a last try for S & P levels, then turn off the heat and stir in the spinach.

○ Ladle into warmed bowls or mugs and Get Better Soon!

HERE'S TO A SPEEDY RECOVERY

Timeline

ANYTIME ON THE DAY OR DAY BEFORE

Poach chick, cool and pick

AN HOUR BEFORE YOU WANT THEM

Start making puffs

Soup can be an anytime-you're-poorly-thing, as it freezes well too

THYME FLATBREADS

PREP: 2 HOURS • COOK: 5 MINS

BEETROOT TZATZIKI

PREP: 5 MINS

TURKISH TURKEY BURGERS (McTURCOS)

PREP: 10 MINS • COOK: 10 MINS

mcturcos

'McTurco!' we shouted when we first bit into these fine flatbreads filled with Middle-Eastern flavours. Deniz, my culinary wing-woman on this book, and I both share a love of food from that part of the world – her by heritage, me by adoption.

And this is like everything that's great about a burger – meat-focused, bread-led with the best tried-and-tested supporting flavours. The beetroot is a good, garish twist to the usual tzatziki, and the input required to make freshly baked flatbread is so worthwhile compared to a shoe-sole pitta. Round it all off with a handful of fresh herbs and a throw of pistachios to enter a world of Bosphorus burger bliss.

THYME FLATBREADS

MAKES 4 FAB FLATTIES

4 tablespoons thyme leaves, picked and roughly chopped

225g plain flour, plus extra for dusting

7g fast-action dried yeast (1 sachet)

1 teaspoon sea salt

½ teaspoon caster sugar

about 130ml warm water

splash of olive oil, plus extra for brushing

○ Put all the dry ingredients (including the thyme) in a food processor, pulse briefly to mix, then with the processor still running pour in the warm water in a steady stream until it looks/feels like wet, sticky breadcrumbs, adding more water if necessary, a teaspoon at a time.

○ Knead on a lightly floured work surface until the dough becomes elastic and smooth (a good 4–5 minutes), then roll into a ball. Pop it into a bowl big enough to allow for a decent rise, then splash on a little olive oil to lightly coat the surface. Cover loosely with a damp cloth and leave to prove somewhere warm ('like an airy cupboard' as my co-cook Deniz says) for 1½–2 hours until it has more or less doubled in size.

○ When you're half an hour or so from McTurk time, preheat the oven to 160°C/140°C fan/gas mark 3 and put a griddle/skillet on to heat up.

○ Scatter a little flour on your work surface and give the dough another quick knead. Bring it back into a ball, cut into quarters and roll each one out to an oval roughly 15 x 20cm. Pile them up with a scattering of flour in between to stop them sticking and drape a tea towel over them whilst you are cooking the burgers (see over the page).

○ Once the burgers are cooked and set aside to rest, brush the first of the flatbreads lightly with olive oil and fling it on the smoking hot griddle. Wait until the flatbread bubbles, poofs up and has markings you approve of on its underside (2–3 minutes), then turn over and cook for the same time on the other side. Once it's ready, wrap it in a tea towel, pop in the oven and get on with cooking the next one, and so on until they're all done.

MAKES
A MEZZE
BOWLFUL

BEETROOT TZATZIKI

120g pickled beetroot (either from
    a vac-pack or jar)

1 clove of garlic, grated or finely
    chopped

zest and juice of ½ lemon

200g Turkish or Greek yogurt

Salt

○ Put the beetroot, garlic, lemon zest and juice in a food processor and
    blitz into little pieces, stopping short of a purée.

○ Tip the yogurt into a bowl, scrape the beetroot mix into it and stir
    together in an aesthetically pleasing swirly way.

○ Season with salt and more lemon juice to taste (depends on the acidity
    of the beetroot).

TURKISH TURKEY BURGERS

FOR 4 (MAKES 8 BABY BURGERS; 2 PER PORTION)

1 small potato, peeled and grated
    on the big holes

1 small courgette, grated on the
    big holes

500g turkey mince

1 spring onion, finely chopped

1–2 red chillies (depending on
    your taste and their ferocity),
    deseeded and finely chopped

1 clove of garlic, finely chopped

½ teaspoon ground cumin

1 egg, beaten

60g fresh white breadcrumbs
    (1 v. thick slice, crusts off,
    whizzed in a food processor),
    + a bit more if the mix still seems
    pretty wet

a small handful (10g) of coriander,
    chopped

a big handful (20g) of mint leaves,
    half chopped, half left whole

a big handful (20g) of flat-leaf
    parsley leaves, half chopped, half
    left whole

1 tablespoon olive oil

S & P

○ Stir the potato and courgette together in a bowl big enough to hold all
    the ingredients. Pick up a big handful of the mix and, over the sink,
    squeeze as hard as you can to extract as much water as possible, then
    put to one side and repeat until the bowl is empty.

○ Give the bowl a quick rinse and dry, then pop the squeezed veg balls
    back in there along with all the other ingredients, except the oil and
    whole leaf herbs.

○ Season with gusto – turkey isn't famed for its flavour so needs a bold
    hand. Mix thoroughly, then divide evenly into eight and shape them
    into little burgerettes 6–7cm across with a bit of a depression in the
    middle (we all know that feeling), which will help them cook more evenly (see
    box opposite).

○ Preheat the oven to 160°C/140°C fan/gas mark 3.

○ Ideally, you'll cook these on a griddle (well, really ideally you'll do it
    over coals/wood outside), but failing both of those a skillet or thick-
    bottomed dry frying pan will do the job fine.

○ Once your chosen equipment is hot, brush each patty lightly with the
    oil and cook for roughly 3–4 minutes a side until lightly browned/bar
    marked, then move onto a small baking tray and pop them in the oven
    whilst you get on with the flatbreads (see previous page).

○ When the flatbreads are all cooked and keeping warm in the oven, have
    a final check that the burgers are done by either inserting a skewer into
    the middle, which should come out hot, or just secretly break one open
    a bit and have a look... they'll never know by the time you've put it all
    together, which brings us to...

TO GO IN THE WRAPS

1 head baby gem, outer leaves only/4 cos leaves, washed

a big handful (40g) of shelled pistachios, crushed with the side of a knife

THE BUILD

(This is easiest/best if you put all the ingredients on the table and folks make their own.)

- Fold the flatbreads in half like an open envelope and lay a leaf or two of lettuce on the bottom.
- Spread with a generous splodge of the tzatziki, then load up with a couple of McTurco's.
- Finish with the whole mint and parsley leaves and a scattering of pistachios, then close the lid and get stuck in sharpish.

ÇOK LEZETLI!!
('BLOODY YUMMY' IN TURKISH!)

WHY THE DIMPLE?

The first reason is purely aesthetic: meat contracts whilst cooking so you can get a bit of a dome in the middle and the dimple helps ensure a nice flat end product.

The second is a bit more scientific: obviously the heat takes longest to penetrate the middle, and using your thumb to make a slight dip in the centre on each side makes it thinner than the outside parts. This means it will take less time to reach a safe temperature, thus avoiding the outside becoming mullered and dry.

It's all about making the best possible food... and not killing anyone.

Timeline

2-ISH HOURS BEFORE
Make dough and prove

ANY TIME IN THIS WINDOW
Knock up beetroot tzatziki
Make and shape burgers

HALF AN HOUR BEFORE NOSH ON
Roll out dough
Griddle burgers
Griddle flatbreads
Build!

Q U I C K

bang-a-gong turkey chow down

TURKEY DRUMMERS

PREP: 30 MINS • COOK: 3ISH HOURS

BACON BREADCRUMBS

PREP: 5 MINS • COOK: 15 MINS

JALAPEÑO CORNBREAD MUFFINS

PREP: 10 MINS • COOK: 15 MINS

There's a fair amount of noise aimed at gastropubs for repopularising all the old, unfashionable cuts of meat and thus driving up their price. Oxtail would be an obvious one, along with flank steak, lamb shanks and pork belly, but for some reason I've yet to see the same fate befall turkey drummers, which is bonkers as pound for pound they're practically free. Damn tasty too, as long as you give them plenty of oven time and flavours to work with.

They look like something that's fallen out of the Flintstones, or that thing that the guy at the beginning of Rank movies used to bang the gong with... which gives you at least half the reason for the recipe title. The other half is a little more of a stretch: DNA-wise, the closest living relative to the T. Rex is the turkey, and what with Marc Bolan being my first male crush, I know all the words to pretty much all their tunes, including the line in 'Get It On' which goes, of course, Bang A Gong. Gedditt??

As for the muffins, to jalapeño or not to jalapeño? It's a tough one: on the one hand, the jalapeños make these muffins really rather special; on the other, kids love cornbread and it seems a bit mean to lace them with what is pure dynamite to most young palates. As a compromise, I usually end up making half a tray with and half without, but any which way you go, don't miss the magic that happens when you dunk them in the soup.

TURKEY DRUMMERS
(WITH A SOUTHERN-STYLE TOMATO SOUP ON THE SIDE)

GOOD FOR 6

IN THE PAN

2 x 400g tins chopped tomatoes

50g tomato purée

3 tablespoons maple syrup

100g tomato ketchup

2 tablespoons Worcestershire sauce

CONTINUED OPPOSITE

○ Preheat the oven to 160°C/140°C fan/gas mark 3.

○ Put a wide pan on the stove over a medium heat and tip in the toms, along with half a tin of water.

○ As it comes up to a simmer, add in all the other pan ingredients, except half of the BBQ sauce, which you need to put aside for later, then once it's bubbling away, turn it off.

○ Meanwhile, get out a big roasting tray and lay the drummers in it. Using a skewer, poke 20–30 deep holes in each of them, going all the way to the bone (this aids deep penetration of flavour, as well as slightly faster and more even cooking) then give them a bit of a season.

* When I first cooked, wrote and re-tested this recipe it was in October/November, and when I asked for a couple of turkey drummers from my butcher I got MASSOOF ones that weighed a kilo each. By the time it came to the photo shoot we were in May, and the ones I got on this occasion weighed just shy of half a kilo each, so I got four instead of two. This recipe is good at any time of year, but in truth I prefer the caveman-like ones, so maybe save this cook for that magic time between Hallowe'en and Christmas.

50ml cider vinegar

½ teaspoon sweet smoked paprika (although I'd sneak it up to 1 teaspoon if there aren't any kids coming to the party, and probs whack some chilli flakes in there too)

500ml chicken stock

150g decent-quality BBQ sauce (I like Sweet Baby Ray's, available in most supermarkets)

1 scant tablespoon salt

IN THE ROASTING TRAY

2kg turkey drummers (see note below left*)

2 large red onions (500g), peeled

2 large carrots (200g), thickly sliced

3 bay leaves

S & P

○ Cut the bottoms off the onions so they sit flat in the tray, then quarter them down towards the root but not through it. Nestle them into the roasting tray, along with the carrots and bay leaves (count them in so you can count them out again later).

○ Tip the hot tomatoey sauce into the roasting tray over the drummers – you need it to come about ⅔–¾ of the way up them, so top up with water if necessary.

○ Foil the tray tightly and put it in the middle of the oven. Depending on the size of the drummers, it'll take anywhere from 1½ to 3 hours to do its thing (I know that's a pretty wide window I've given you there, but the note on the opposite page explains why). You'll know when they're done because the sauce will have reduced and thickened, the turkey flesh will have pulled back from the bone, and when you stick a skewer into the middle of the thickest part, it should come out hot.

○ Use the same foil to line your grill tray and preheat it to medium. Move the drummers into the grill tray and brush all over with the other half of the BBQ sauce.

○ As the grill is coming up to speed, get on with finishing the soup: pick out the bay leaves and, in two batches, blend the contents of the roasting tray until totally smooth. It makes a fair amount and is thick too: enough for tonight's supper plus a couple of lunches to boot, and beyond if you choose to let it down with a bit of hot water, which isn't a bad idea... (and neither is a bit of seasoning).

○ Back to the drummers: grill for about 5ish minutes, depending on the ferocity of your grill, until nicely glazed all over.

○ Put the bacon breadcrumbs on a plate or tray and gently roll the glazed drummers in them, then move onto your presentation dish (an upturned gong is ideal) and serve up with warm muffins and cups of soup.

Timeline

FEW HOURS BEFORE
Get drummers going

ANY TIME IN THIS WINDOW
Bang out the breadcrumbs (they're happy to sit but saves you a job for later)

HALF AN HOUR BEFORE DRUMMERS OUT
Start making your muffs (to go in about 10ish mins before turkey comes out)

ONCE TURKEY OUT
Grill on

Blend soup

Glaze and grill drummers

Roll in breadcrumbs

Enjoy, y'all!

BACON BREADCRUMBS

150g fresh, white breadcrumbs

3 tablespoons plain oil (like vegetable or sunflower)

170g smoked streaky bacon, finely diced (the smaller the better)

20g butter

freshly ground black pepper

○ Preheat the oven to 160°C/140°C fan/gas mark 3.

○ Spread the breadcrumbs out on a baking tray and pop in the oven to dry out to the point where they could be called stale and a bit old looking, as opposed to white, soft and fluffy, but don't go as far as desiccated and browning – anywhere up to 10 minutes, depending on your oven.

○ Put a heavy-based wide frying pan over a medium–high heat and pour in the oil. As it's warming up, do a bit of *mise en place* by sitting a sieve over a metal heatproof bowl and put this next to the stove.

○ Once the oil is hot, tip in the bacon and keep frying and stirring through the attractive golden stage; hold your nerve as you need it to properly dry out to browned nuggets in order to be crunchy, not chewy, later.

○ When you're happy with your Baco Bits, tip them into the sieve straight away to stop them becoming Burnt Bits.

○ Put the pan back on the heat (no washing), pour in the oil from the bacon, melt the butter in it and chuck in the breadcrumbs.

○ Over a medium–high heat, stir pretty constantly until the breadcrumbs are an all-over golden colour, then tip into a food processor along with the bacon, and pulse in short spurts until it looks how you'd like your bacon breadcrumbs to look (my advice is to head for a slightly chunky crumb, not teensy weensy – better look and bite).

○ Move onto a tray lined with kitchen paper to degrease as it cools, and give it a good crack of black pepper – no salt required.

JALAPEÑO CORNBREAD MUFFINS

140g cornmeal

140g plain flour

35g caster sugar

2 teaspoons baking powder

250ml milk

1 egg, beaten

100g butter, melted

200g frozen sweetcorn, thawed

1 teaspoon salt and a few good
cracks of the pepper mill

3 jalapeños, 2 chopped, 1 sliced
(this is enough to fire up the lot,
so if you're making half kiddy-
friendly, then go for 2)

extra butter, to serve

○ Preheat the oven to 190°C/170°C fan/gas mark 5 and grease a muffin
tin with a bit of melted butter – around a tablespoon should do it.

○ Put all the dry ingredients in a mixing bowl, give them a quick shuffle-
mix with a fork, then pour in the wet ingredients including the melted
butter. Use light movements with the fork to just combine into a pretty
dense batter.

○ Mix in the sweetcorn and seasoning. Now's the time to split your
batter if there are kiddlies involved, before stirring through the
chopped jalapeños, keeping the slices for the top to illustrate what
lies beneath.

○ Spoon the mix equally into the muffin tray, and bake for 15–20 minutes
in the middle of the oven until golden brown, then use the old skewer-
comes-out-clean trick to see if they're ready.

○ Eat warm, with plenty of butter, and don't forget to dunk them in
the soup.

partridge
(no pear tree)

SLOE-BRAISED RED CABBAGE
WITH PRUNES & BACON

PREP: 5 MINS • COOK: 3 HOURS • LEAVE: OVERNIGHT

ROAST PARTRIDGE

PREP: 5 MINS • COOK: 20 MINS

GAME CHIPS

PREP: 10 MINS • COOK: 5 MINS

This is one of the most natural threesomes in the book: a little roast game bird, a pile of slow-cooked boozy, bacony cabbage and some crisp, salty game chips on the side.

It just may be one of the finest meals ever... deceivingly simple too.

ROAST PARTRIDGE

1 tablespoon olive oil

2 partridge (about 250–300g each)

a few sprigs of fresh thyme or rosemary

120ml Madeira or medium-sweet sherry (like your Gran's i.e. Bristol Cream)

S & P

○ Preheat the oven to 220°C/200°C fan/gas mark 7. Put a heavy-based frying pan or skillet big enough for the birds over a high heat.

○ Pour in the oil and whilst it's heating up, season the partridges well on all sides and inside too. Stick the thyme or rosemary in the cavities.

○ Once the oil is smoking hot, lay the birds in, breast-side down, inclining them to favour one side (they can quite happily lean against each other for support).

○ Give them a minute or two, then alter their position so the other breast is favoured, and when that's nicely coloured, turn them onto first one leg side to brown and then the other.

○ Finish this part of the operation with them on their backs, breasts up, then put in the oven on the top shelf for 10–12 minutes, depending on which end of the weight window your birds are.

○ When time's up, take them out and check they're cooked by sticking something slender (like a skewer) into the top of the leg joint. Keep it there for a count of 5 seconds, then put it to your top lip: if it's cold, put them back in the oven; if it's hot, you've mullered them already; what you want is for the tip of that skewer to be just warm at this stage, as they will carry on cooking as they rest.

○ Once you're happy that the partridge are spot-on, move them onto a plate to rest for 3–4 minutes.

○ Dispose of the fat in the pan in an environmentally friendly fashion, then put it back on the hob over a medium heat. Pour in the booze and reduce over a couple of minutes to a thin glaze. Give this quickest of sauces a touch of seasoning and when you serve the birds, spoon it all over them.

SLOE-BRAISED RED CABBAGE
WITH PRUNES & BACON

2 tablespoons olive oil

1 onion, roughly chopped

130g lardons, preferably smoked

1kg red cabbage (roughly
    1 supermarket one or ½ a big 'un
    from the market), core cut out
    and roughly cut into 2cm slices

3–5 cloves, depending on size and
    how much you like them

¼ teaspoon ground allspice

100g prunes, stoned

3 tablespoons marmalade

80ml (5 tablespoons) sherry
    vinegar

80ml (5 tablespoons) maple syrup

300ml sloe gin

S & P

○ Preheat the oven to 150°C/130°C fan/gas mark 2. Put a wide, ovenproof pan (with a lid that fits) on a medium–high heat and pour the oil into it.

○ Once hot, sauté the onion and lardons until just beginning to brown, then chuck in the cabbage. Continue to fry and turn as you add the cloves and allspice.

○ Season well, then when all the cabbage is glossy – after about 5 minutes – stir in the prunes, marmalade, vinegar, maple syrup and two-thirds of the sloe gin.

○ Put the lid on and chuck in the oven for 3 hours, popping by for a quick visit and a shuffle halfway through if you happen to be in the vicinity – no biggie if you're not.

○ When its sojourn in the oven is over, give it a good turning over and leave for a bit of a rest to come together... on the doorstep overnight is ideal.

○ As partridge time approaches, reheat the cabbage briefly on the hob, then turn it off, stir in the remainder of the sloe gin and have a last look at the seasoning.

Timeline

**WELL IN ADVANCE
(PREF DAY
BEFORE)**

Make cabbage

**HALF AN HOUR
FROM SERVING**

Get yourself ready for the game chips (i.e. spuds peeled, slicing tool located – but don't slice them yet; oil in pan, gently heating)

Get partridge in.

Once the birds are in the oven, turn the oil up to full and get going with the the spud-slicing and frying

(Not forgetting to reheat cabbage...)

GAME CHIPS

about 1 litre vegetable oil,
   for deep-frying
600g chipping spuds, peeled
salt, to taste

○ Just before you start cooking the partridge, pour the oil into a big, high-sided pan – think Le Creuset casseroler or something like that – and put it on a low-ish heat. Peel the spuds and choose your slicing implement: you need to slice them thinner than a knife can, so if you own a mandolin now's the moment, and if you don't, then reach for your trusty box grater. A mandolin inevitably does a tidier job, but actually I ended up preferring the result from the slicing blade on the side of the grater as those raggedy edges make for fabulous crispy bits.

○ Don't start cutting them, though, until the birds are in the oven, then crank the oil up and as it comes up to speed slice away.

○ Check the oil is hot enough by dropping in a single slice of spud; if it fizzles furiously, you're good to go, so quickly slide in about a third of the spuds and immediately give it a stir to stop them sticking together.

○ Keep them moving round for pretty much all of the 2–3 minutes they'll take to turn a deep golden brown, only briefly breaking away to prepare a landing tray lined with kitchen paper.

○ When you're happy with the colour, use a slotted spoon to lift them onto the tray. Season with salt, then put in the oven (which will still be hot from the partridge) and get the next lot going. Once they're all cooked and crispy, don't mess about – game on!

THE CURRY

PREP: 30 MINS · COOK: 3 HOURS

SEASONED RICE

COOK: 15 MINS

COLD-INFUSED JASMINE & LIME LEAF TEA

PREP: 5 MINS · LEAVE: OVERNIGHT

yellow duck curry

I know what you're all thinking: 'Sounds yummy, but it's got too many ingredients'. And whilst you're right about the first part, you're wrong about the second. This dish has got just the right amount of ingredients to make it fabulous – not one extra puppy in there, for real. And anyway, as a reward for taking on a recipe that I do appreciate is not exactly boil-in-the-bag easy, the two sidekick cooks are both simple and gentle – there to support and enhance. The word is cold-infusing tea leaves calmly overnight renders a cleaner, lighter, purer flavour as they haven't been subjected to boiling water: all very West Coast.

For those of you who are capsaicin-worshippers (like me) you might also want to quickly knock up the Non-approved Nuclear Explosion on page 79 (a Korean-ish chilli pickle), as this curry is more of a stroke of the earlobe than a clap on the back.

As bright as it is deep, and fragrant as it is flavoursome, this is start -to-finish fun to make and eat. A proper cook's curry. (And yup, for the record, I am aware this threesome is actually a Slow Slow Quick... no need to write in, thanks!)

THE CURRY

FOR 4 ENTHUSIASTS OR 6 MODERATES

2kg whole duck, legs and breasts removed (this is very simple to do, but if you don't fancy it, ask the butcher, who will do it at lightning speed)

S & P

FOR THE STOCK

1 onion, peeled and halved

2 carrots, washed and broken in half

2 star anise

½ thumb of fresh ginger, peeled

3ish lime leaves

1 teaspoon coriander seeds (if you happen to have any knocking around)

FOR THE PASTE

1 tablespoon ground turmeric or 20g fresh, unpeeled, washed, gnarly bits trimmed and very

roughly chopped + 1 teaspoon ground (adds depth of flavour and colour too)

2 green chillies, tops off and cut into thirds (seeds in)

200g shallots, peeled and quartered

6ish cloves of garlic, peeled

2 sticks lemongrass, tops and bottoms trimmed, then thinly sliced (1cm)

50g galangal, washed, unpeeled, trimmed of any tough bits and roughly chopped (or if you can't get it, sub 30g fresh ginger and prep in the same way)

120ml peanut or vegetable oil + 1 tablespoon light soy sauce (for breast marinade)

THE VEG SECTION

½ large or 1 small cauliflower, cut into florets

300g white cabbage or ½ small Savoy, roughly diced into 2cm pieces

150g mushrooms (chesnut/Paris/button), washed, destalked and torn in half/ quarters, depending on size

1 red pepper, deseeded and chunkily diced

TO FINISH

200g block creamed coconut (comes in a packet, not tinned)

a tin of coconut milk

150g sugar snap peas

2 tablespoons light soy sauce

juice of 1 lime, plus wedges to serve

a handful of Thai basil leaves or coriander, very roughly chopped

1 bunch of spring onions, thinly sliced on an angle

YELLOW DUCK CURRY CONT...

○ Trim any large bits of fat off the duck carcass, then whack it in half. (And if, like me, you're waste-phobic, render the fatty off-cuts down for the next time you make roasties... it lasts in the fridge for millennia.) Put it, plus the legs and all the other stock ingredients, in a big pan and pour on cold water to just cover (around 2 litres). Pop the breasts to one side for now, and if the bird came with giblets, put the neck in the stock, and the heart, kidneys and liver with the breasts.

○ Bring to the boil, then reduce the heat so just steaming – no lid. There's no action required in the stock pot now for 1½ hours, so crack on with a few bits of prep: first off, make the paste by whizzing everything together in a blender until smooth.

○ Next up prep the duck breasts: lay them on your board, skin-side down, and trim off all the fat protruding from under the flesh (it's good stuff, but just too much for this dish, so put it with the rest of the fat trimmed from the carcass for rendering) ...or you can cut the whole lot off, depending how you feel about duck fat.

○ Slice the breasts widthways into 1cm-thick pieces, then take 2 tablespoons of the paste plus 1 tablespoon of light soy and use your hands to thoroughly coat them in it.

○ If you're a gibletter, trim the heart, liver and kidneys of all fat and sinew, chop them roughly and mix in with the marinating breasts. Cover the lot and put in the fridge.

○ The last one to knock off is prepping the veg – just a bit of light knife work, but better to get it done now, as once the stock is reduced it all happens pretty quickly.

○ After the stock's been on for 1½ hours, lift out the legs (and neck if it's lurking in there) and put them aside to cool. Now whack up the heat to full pelt: keep it on a very busy rolling boil until it's reduced down to just north of 500ml, which takes around 40–60 minutes, depending on your pan and ferocity of your hob. When you reckon the stock has hit its magic mark (500–600ml), strain it and bin the solids.

○ Once the legs (and neck) are cool enough to handle, pick the meat off and roughly shred, chucking out the skin and bones, then toss briefly with a good pinch of salt.

○ You are now ready to curry: stick a large, wide pan on a high heat and wait for it to get properly hot. Individually and quickly lay down as many slices of breast (and any gibletty bits) it takes to cover the bottom of the pan in one layer: you may or may not be able to do this in one lot. As soon as the base is covered start turning the first ones (i.e. after just a minute) - they're going to stick as there was no oil in the pan, but don't stress, you're just trying to give them a quick seal. Cook just as briefly on the other side, then get them out of there. Repeat if necessary, waiting for the pan to get good and hot again before going in with the rest of the slices/giblets.

○ Turn the heat down low, tip in the paste, stir and fry for about 10 minutes, lowering in the block of coconut cream half way through to melt and mix in. Then pour in the coconut milk, turn the heat up to medium, and stir until smooth.

○ Chuck in the cauli, cabbage, mushrooms and red pepper. Season, then take a bit of time and attention to coat the veg in the fragrant sauce. Pop a lid on, reduce the heat right down and leave the veg to start to soften (but not cook through) for about 10 minutes, with the odd stir and turn.

○ Now add the reduced stock and picked leg (and neck) meat; put the lid back on and bring to a gentle simmer. Once the veg are cooked – just another few minutes – stir in the breast slices + giblets and sugar snaps. Bring back to a simmer, then turn off immediately and finish to taste with soy sauce and lime juice. Now you're good to go my friend, just don't forget the spring onions, chopped herbs and lime wedges as you ladle out the love.

SEASONED RICE

FOR 4

300g long-grain rice

¾ teaspoon salt

2 tablespoons rice wine vinegar

2 teaspoons mirin

To make it for 6 people, increase the amounts as follows:

450g long-grain rice
1 teaspoon salt
3 tablespoons rice wine vinegar
1 tablespoon mirin

This is the base recipe – augment and enhance as you wish, for example, by putting some seaweed in with the rice as it cooks, or stirring through black sesame seeds after cooking.

○ Cook the rice as per the packet instructions. In a little bowl, stir the salt into the vinegar and mirin until roughly dissolved.

○ Once the rice is cooked, drain for a minute, then run under the cold tap for just a few seconds to stop it overcooking (you don't want to cool it too much, though, as rice absorbs more flavour when warm/hot).

○ Tip it back into the pan (not on the heat), pour on the seasoning and mix together using a fork to keep it fluffy. Taste and adjust to your liking.

Timeline

NIGHT BEFORE
Get tea cold-infusing

3-ISH HOURS BEFORE THE EVENT
Start curry (or you can make paste & do recipe to point of reduced stock the day before)

ONCE STOCK REDUCED
Put rice on and finish curry

20–30 MINS LATER
You're all up!

COLD-INFUSED JASMINE & LIME LEAF TEA

MAKES 1 LITRE (ENOUGH FOR 6 ZEN FOLK TO HAVE A COUPLE OF SMALL BOWLS/TEACUPS EACH, OR 4 LONG DRINKS OVER ICE)

1 litre tap water (but of course if you're all about purity, use mineral)

4 jasmine teabags or 3 tablespoons loose pearls

4 lime leaves (my top tip is to buy a load and stick them in the freezer where they keep very happily for months)

lime wedges and ice (if serving cold)

○ Pour a litre of water into a jug or large jar, then stir in the tea and lime leaves.

○ Leave in the fridge overnight and strain before serving either warmed up, or over ice with lime (just let it float in there rather than squeezing it, as we don't want to overpower those gentle flavours).

CHICKEN & OTHER BIRDS

chapter two
lamb

When it comes to slow cooking, lamb has to be the instinctive go-to meat. It's Number One in my mind when you want to put it in the oven and walk away, and folks all over the world have been doing just that for millennia.

Whilst the recipes in this chapter ostensibly illustrate that geographical stretch – from a madras of the sub continent to a French-inspired super-slow cooked *gigot* – on closer inspection you may notice that there's one global cuisine that weaves its way into certainly most, and arguably all, of the collectives. When Carly Simon sang that 'Nobody does it better' she may well have been talking about how those culinary genii on the eastern shores of the Med handle their lamb. From Greece through Turkey, round to Lebanon and beyond, the indigenous flavours just go effortlessly and naturally with this sweetest of meats.

Subtle but penetrating spices; nuts, fruit, lots of herbs and super-fresh salads all support and enhance the particular taste profile of muscle and fat that only lamb can offer.

And it's not just the ingredients but also their age-old hand-me-down techniques that suit the species: at the risk of generalisation, the two ways of crossing the line from raw to cooked most associated with that part of the world are the charcoal grill and the low and slow oven. Both of which provide a suitably scrumptious send off to Larry the Lamb's little life!

lamb
breast

lamb breast

CRISP BREAST
AKA 'LAMB MALPLAQUETS'

PREP: 4 HOURS • LEAVE: OVERNIGHT • FINISHING: 30 MINS

PUY LENTIL TABBOULEH

PREP: 15 MINS • COOK: 20 MINS (SIMULTANEOUSLY)

POM-MOL ONION RELISH

PREP: 10 MINS • COOK: 20 MINS

BUBBLE & BAA

PREP: 20 MINS • COOK: 20 MINS

OK – I'm just going to put it out there: this is one of my proudest moments in the book. No getting round it takes a bit of time/planning, but isn't that what slow cooking is all about? And believe me, when you get to the finishing line, it's more worth it than you can possibly imagine.

The breast is our hero – dirt cheap per kilo, but that's no reflection of the result, simply that it takes a bit of time and care to bring it to fruition. Pricing of meat is just a continuation of the sad but true equation we all live our lives by these days: time = money. As a head's up, you won't find this cut lurking on the supermarket shelves; it's a butcher's job for sure.

Enough of the boohoo and let me sell this baby to you: the transformation of the lamb is really rather special – you may not be able to make a silk purse out of a sow's ear, but you can turn something that's normally thrown to the dogs into a dinner fit for Fay or Jay or Giles or Marina.

The breast of our figurehead is leading the charge, backed up by her two Chief Mates, who are both supporting and enhancing. Truly a spectacular finish from such humble beginnings, and whilst we're talking antithesis, after what is essentially a Middle-Eastern feast, it feels nicely down to earth to finish our cook-athon with a bit of proper Britishness – Bubble & Baa (you heard it here first).

CRISP BREAST (AKA 'LAMB MALPLAQUETS')

SUPPER/WEEKEND LUNCH FOR 6, PLUS ENOUGH FOR THE BUBBLE & BAA

2.5–3kg lamb breast (which can be 2 or 3 pieces, depending on the time of year)

4 banana shallots (or 8 regular ones), very roughly chopped

2 carrots, cut into chunky pieces

5 cloves of garlic, crushed, then peeled

100ml cider vinegar

100g runny honey

○ Preheat the oven to 160°C/140°C fan/gas mark 3. Season the lamb breasts well and pack into a large roasting tray with the shallots, carrots and garlic fitting in wherever they can (and if it's rammed in there just sit them on top; the lamb will shrink as it cooks).

○ Pour on the vinegar and honey, plus enough chicken stock to just about cover the meat – it doesn't matter if there's a bit sticking out – then submerge the bay and rosemary.

○ Cover tightly with foil and put on the bottom shelf of the oven for 4 hours, by which point the meat will be super-tender.

around 1 litre chix stock, plus or minus 250ml depending on your tray and lamb size

3 bay leaves

3 sprigs of rosemary, leaves picked and chopped

FOR BREADCRUMBING

2 handfuls of plain flour, seasoned

2 eggs, beaten with 2 tablespoons water

200g panko or regular breadcrumbs

50g butter

a little olive oil, for frying

2 lemons, 1 for juicing and t'other for serving

S & P

○ Lift the veg out with a slotted spoon and set aside. Strain the juice and fat into a separate bowl (picking out the bay) and then leave all three components to cool to room temperature. The veggies now go into the fridge overnight, as do the liquids, so transfer to a smaller bowl/jar if necessary. Both of these are down payments for the slightly epic Bubble and Baa that will follow a meal or two after the main shebang.

○ Whilst the breasts are still warm enough to be supple (i.e. don't let them go rock-hard cold by leaving them on the doorstep in the middle of winter), pull out the bones and cartilage, as well as the intramuscular layers of connective tissue (you'll know what I mean when you get there). To be frank, it's a little bit of an operation, but take it slow and steady, tugging and coaxing out anything that you wouldn't want to put in your mouth, whilst trying to keep the breast's form in tact as opposed to letting it fall apart into a shapeless pile of meat. Your pile of debris should be roughly half (or even a bit more) the size of what's left of usable meat, hence the reason why lamb breasts are quite so cheap...

○ Line a small roasting tray (about 30 x 20 x 5cm) with greaseproof paper, then carefully move the lamb pieces into it. Scavenge the bottom of the tray they were cooked in for any good nuggets of meat that have been left behind (this is for the Bubble & Baa), nicking a bit from the main pile of meat if needed to top it up to around 200g/a small bowlful.

○ The aim of the game now is to jigsaw puzzle what's left of the three breasts into one flat rectangle of meat. It's going to be compressed overnight, which will kind of glue it together, so just do the best job you can to patchwork it into one piece and don't get too obsessional about it.

○ When you're happy with your meat quilt, lay another piece of greaseproof on top, and find something flat (ideally another similar-sized roasting tray) that can act as a pressure-dispersing barrier between the meat and the Great Weight you're about to put on top of it (the more snugly it fits inside the roasting tray the better). Now go in search of the Great Weight – a foil-wrapped brick always works if you can't see anything else – then put in the fridge and leave to compact overnight.

○ This penultimate stage is best done ahead of time as it's a little messy (for a change). Lift the bottom piece of greaseproof and set down on a chopping board. Carefully peel off both bits of paper so as to not break up your slab of meat, then cut it into 8–12 similar-sized shapes (I prefer irregular of course, hence the subtitle of 'malplaquets', but rectangles/squares also work).

CONTINUED OVER THE PAGE

Timeline

DAY BEFORE (AND NOT STARTING LESS THAN 6HRS BEFORE YOU WANT TO STOP COOKING FOR THE DAY)

Cook, cool, pick and press lamb

ANYTIME ON THE DAY

Make the pom mol relish

Make the lentil tabbouleh

Cut and breadcrumb lamb

30 MINS OR SO BEFORE THE BELL

Preheat oven and fry the lamb

NEXT DAY (OR EVEN THE ONE AFTER) ...

Bubble & baa

CRISP BREAST CONT...

○ Set up your breadcrumbing station in the time-honoured fashion: four wide shallow vessels of some sort, the first with seasoned flour, the second with eggs beaten with water, the third has the breadcrumbs and the last is your landing mat for when they're done. My advice is to take three shapes at a time through the whole breadcrumbing procedure, then rub your fingertips together to get off the sticky crumbs and go again.

○ When they're all done, put them in the fridge until you're half an hour or so away from serving, then take them out and turn the oven on to 160°C/140°C fan/gas mark 3.

○ Put a wide, heavy-based frying pan on a medium heat, melt the butter in the oil until fizzling, then lay in as many pieces of breadcrumbed lamb as fit nicely without overcrowding.

○ Turn when golden underneath (3–4 minutes), then fry to a similar colour on the other side. Get a tray lined with kitchen paper ready and, once the lamb pieces are done, lift them onto it and put in the oven whilst you get on with the next batch, adding a bit more butter and oil if needed.

○ When they're all done, hit them with a good sprinkling of sea salt and a fair squeeze of lemon, then serve up with the tabbouleh, onion relish, more lemons on the side and ann air of expectation.

POM-MOL ONION RELISH

2 tablespoons olive oil

700g onions, medium diced

2 cloves of garlic, chopped

1 tablespoon rosemary leaves, chopped

100ml balsamic vinegar

100ml pomegranate molasses

a little honey, to taste (optional)

S & P

○ Pour the oil into a wide saucepan and once it's hot, tip in the onions.

○ Fry over a brisk heat, stirring regularly, until they start to turn translucent, then stir in the garlic and rosemary.

○ Carry on frying for a few minutes as they release their aromas, then pour in the vinegar and pomegranate molasses.

○ Reduce the heat to a steady simmer, stirring from time to time, until the liquids have reduced to just a coating consistency and the onions are gorgeously glossy, about 20–25 minutes.

○ Season to taste, stirring in a touch of honey if you feel it needs it (a totally personal thing) and serve at room temp or just above it.

PUY LENTIL TABBOULEH

FOR THE LENTILS

250g dried puy lentils

1 fat clove of garlic, minced

3 tablespoons extra virgin olive oil

2 tablespoons red wine vinegar

S & P

FOR EVERYTHING ELSE

30g flat-leaf parsley, leaves picked and roughly chopped

30g mint, leaves picked and roughly chopped

150g cherry tomatoes, halved

5 spring onions, thinly sliced

160g pomegranate seeds (roughly ½ a pom if you're doing it yourself, which is, of course, tastier)

juice of 1 lemon

4 tablespoons extra virgin olive oil

○ Tip the lentils into a saucepan, cover with cold water (no salt) and bring to the boil with a lid on.

○ Take the lid off and turn down to a busy simmer until they are cooked, anything from 15–20 minutes, then drain and spread out on a baking tray.

○ Quick as you can whilst they're still steaming hot, stir in the garlic and dress with the olive oil, vinegar plus a good amount of salt and pepper, then leave to soak up the flavours as they cool.

○ Whilst the lentils are cooking then cooling, get on with preparing everything else – the herbs, toms, spring onions and seeding the pomegranate (unless you cheated and bought them ready done, which is fair enough but tbh is never as good).

○ Put them all into a mixing bowl, saving a few pom seeds for the top, then once the lentils are at room temp, tip them in too.

○ Mix briskly, dress with lemon juice and olive oil, then season well to taste. Spoon into a high pile on a suitably pretty dish and crown with the last of the pom seeds.

BUBBLE & BAA

400g mashing spuds, peeled and quartered/halved

150g toughish greens of any type (such as a small head of spring greens or hispi, or a few leaves of savoy/cavolo nero)

the lamb you'd set aside (about 200g), plus the braising veg, roughly chopped

a handful of plain flour, seasoned

2 tablespoons olive oil

50g butter

juices from cooking the lamb breasts

4 eggs

S & P

IF YOU POSSIBLY CAN HAVE THE FORETHOUGHT, THE BUBBLE AND BAA IS BEST IF THE MASH AND GREENS COMBO IS LEFT TO COOL COMPLETELY BEFORE MAKING; EVEN BETTER IF IT'S MADE THE DAY BEFORE, LIKE IN THE ORIGINS OF THIS DISH'S NAMESAKE.

○ Get your mash on: put the spuds into cold water with a pinch of salt, cover, bring to the boil, then take the lid off and reduce to a busy simmer.

○ Whilst the spuds are cooking, shred/chop the greens. When you reckon the spuds are 5 minutes from being ready (don't overcook them as this makes for a soggy mix to work with later), drop the greens into the water, pushing them under the surface, then stick the lid back on.

○ When a knife goes into the potatoes without resistance and the greens have softened, tip it all into a colander to drain and leave to steam-dry somewhere cool (another doorstep moment) until properly cold.

○ Preheat the oven to 200°C/180°C fan/gas mark 6. Put the spuds, plus greens, into a big bowl and crush roughly to break up (best with the hands so the gluten doesn't become overworked). Chuck in the lamb, veg and some seasoning; stir briskly to mix, then divide into four thick patties. Tip the flour onto a plate and lightly coat on both sides.

○ Reach for your heavy-based ovenproof pan again, and put it over a high heat. Pour in the oil, melt half the butter in it and when it starts to fizzle and brown lay in the patties. Fry for 2–3 minutes until the far side of golden brown, then turn them over and put in the oven.

○ Now turn your attention to yesterday's cooking juices: scrape off the solid white fat and spoon the brown jelly underneath into a little pan, taking care to leave behind the bits of detritus that have sunk to the bottom. You can either bubble it down to reduce or not, but this is an English dish, so in your mind think more loose gravy than sticky jus.

○ After 10-ish minutes, once a skewer inserted into the middle comes out hot-ish, take the Bubble and Baa out of the oven and shifty them onto some kitchen paper to degrease. Briefly and carefully wipe the pan out with a bit more kitchen roll, then put back on the hob over a medium heat (please don't touch the handle). Turn the oven off, but pop your plates in it now to warm up in the residual heat.

○ Melt the remaining butter in the pan and crack in the eggs. You can see where this is going now: bubble in middle of plate, egg on top, juice all around. Yum.

lamb
cutlets

lamb cutlets

The slow aspect to this is that these guys really do benefit from a proper marinade... all that exposed flesh makes them a sponge for flavour.

Ideally it's an overnighter, but if you're pushed for time, then 3–4 hours at room temperature, covered, should do the trick.

By the way, you can also do this with loin chops, which taste just as good and are cheaper, but in reality aren't quite as handsome.

This dish is pure Med, and comes to you from a Moroccan called Chas who has a fondness for Sicily, but whose heart lies in Turkish Cyprus.

ROSEMARY GRILLED CUTLETS

MAINS FOR 4: WORKS WELL AS A LUNCH DISH AS WELL AS SUPS

12 lamb cutlets... or loin chops

salt (at point of cooking)

FOR THE MARINADE

couple of sprigs of rosemary, leaves picked and finely chopped

2 cloves of garlic, chopped

2 tablespoons extra virgin olive oil

plenty of freshly ground black pepper (but NO SALT)

○ Put the cutlets into a container that they can spend the night in.

○ Mix together all the ingredients for the marinade in a little bowl, then spread over the cutlets, using your hands to make sure that every meaty surface is coated. Cover, put in the fridge and leave overnight.

○ An hour before serving, get the lamb out to come up to room temp.

○ When you're 15 minutes away, heat up a griddle, skillet/frying pan or, even better, fire up the barbie – I wouldn't do them under the grill as you won't get that seal that happens with sharp-contact-high-heat.

○ Whilst your cooking equipment is getting searingly hot, season the cutlets on both sides and, if you're cooking inside, take whatever precautions you can not to set off your smoke alarm (doors, windows, extraction, tea towels, leaf blowers and chanting all come to mind).

○ Load as many cutlets as you can in a single layer onto your cooking vessel (if you're using a frying pan, keep it dry – no oil). Cook for 3 minutes on the first side and 2 minutes on the second for pink, which is as it should be (take into account this first batch is going to have a longer rest so will carry on cooking).

○ Cover with foil and keep on the stovetop to stay warm whilst you get on with the next lot, cooking them for a fraction longer on both sides.

○ When they're done, put them on top of the others (gives batch one a little blast of heat), and put the foil back over them for a couple of minutes to rest before serving.

PISTACHIO PESTO

MAKES A JAM JARFUL

100g pistachios, (shelled weight)

1 clove of garlic, minced

80g flat-leaf parsley (renders about 20g picked leaves)

1 lemon

10g Parmesan, grated

75ml extra virgin olive oil

small splash (about a teaspoon) of vinegar – ideally sherry, but red wine also works

S & P

○ Put the pistachios in a food processor and briefly pulse to chunkily chop them. Tip into a little bowl, then replace with the garlic, parsley, zest of the whole lemon and juice of half.

○ Blitz until the parsley is pretty finely chopped, then chuck in the Parmo and give it the quickest of pulses to combine but so there are still discernible bits of cheese (I like my pesto on the coarse side...).

○ Scrape it into a bowl, then stir in the pistachios, olive oil, vinegar and seasoning to taste.

TOMATO, CANNELLINI & OREGANO SALAD

SERVES 4

½ red onion, finely sliced

juice of ½ lemon

600g best vine-ripened tomatoes (a mix of cherry and larger works well, but deffo not essential)

400g tin cannellini beans, drained and rinsed

3 tablespoons fresh oregano (about 15g on the stalk), leaves picked – if you can't get fresh, you can sub this for ½ teaspoon dried, but do try to get fresh – it's worth it

2 tablespoons red wine vinegar

3–4 tablespoons extra virgin olive oil, plus extra for serving

plenty of S & P

○ In a small bowl macerate the onion slices in the lemon juice for a few minutes so they soften and mellow a bit; the longer you leave them in there the more tame and less overpowering they become.

○ Cut the cherry tomatoes in half and dice the larger ones to a similar size, then scrape the toms and their escaped juices from your board into the salad tossing bowl-to-be.

○ Now put all the other ingredients in there too, including the lemon juice from the onions.

○ Season well and toss gently to avoid turning the beans into mush – no piece of equipment can do this as sensitively as your hands.

○ Taste to check seasoning and serve up with a slosh more olive oil on the top.

Timeline

DAY BEFORE
Marinate cutlets

AN HOUR+ BEFORE THE EVENT
Get lamb out to come up to room temp
Knock up pesto
Then make the tom salad

LAST UP
Grill cutlets

7:70 leg of lamb

7:70
(7-HOUR LEG OF LAMB WITH 70 CLOVES OF GARLIC)

PREP: 20 MINS • COOK: 7 HOURS

ALPINE TATTIES

PREP: 5 MINS • COOK: 25 MINS

(TOMORROW'S) MOROCCAN-SPICED FREEKEH

PREP: 5 MINS • COOK: 20 MINS

Having been a keen cook as a youngster, it wasn't until I decided to take it up as a profession that things got serious, and as my college of choice was Le Cordon Bleu, I mean really serious. Who knew that it was so important to have seven perfect sides on your turned veg (which meant that over half the raw material went into the bin), or that a lobster had to be cut in half whilst it was alive to achieve a true Thermidor?

Needless to say, I spent most of my time in the rather good pub next door, but there were a few standout, memorable dishes for me, and one of them was a 'Gigot aux Sept Heures' – 7-hour leg of lamb. Soft, sexy, spoonable and, above all, real food – not cut and contorted, but just left to be. It was beautiful. And all I've done here is resurrect it 25 years later, with an extra 65 cloves of garlic.

The result is nothing short of epic, thanks largely to the hilariously named 'dead dough'...

I've borrowed the Alpine Tatties that earned their place in this book through the Austrian Tafelspitz on page 80, as they're just the perfect carb to go with the super-rich lamb. (And after all, it's just a skippity hop along the Alps from Austria to Southern France.)

And if you're going to invest 7 hours of 'lecky bills on this baby, I'd really try not to miss out on the Moroccan-spiced Freekeh: a gift of a dish from me to you. The result is extraordinarily gentle and sublimely deep for such ridiculously little input.

No really, it's my pleasure!

7:70 (7-HOUR LEG OF LAMB WITH 70 CLOVES OF GARLIC)

2 tablespoons olive oil

a small leg of lamb, anywhere
between 1.4–2kg on the bone*
– ask the butcher to remove the
H-bone (the one at the hip joint)
knuckle it, trim off most, but not
all, of the surface fat and then
tie it

70 cloves of garlic (6–8 bulbs
depending on the size), peeled

3 fat carrots, peeled and cut into 3

4 banana shallots, cut into 6

300ml white wine

1.5l chicken stock

3 bay leaves

10ish stalks of thyme, tied together
with string

S & P

FOR THE DEAD DOUGH

*(multiply this recipe by half again if
using a 30cm pan, e.g. nearer 2kg
leg – see note below*)*

300g plain flour, plus extra
for dusting

pinch of salt

1 egg (if you are multiplying the
recipe by half again, just go for
2 eggs)

100ml water

*If the leg is no more than 1.5kg, you'll be able
to get it in a standard hob-safe casseroling
pan 25cm across and 10cm deep, but for a 2kg
leg, you'll need one more like 30cm across,
which must also be deep enough for the lid
to sit flat once the joint is in, so we're talking
really quite a big pan. Apart from stockpots
and jam pans, it's pretty much the biggest one
I own, and I have a fair few pans...

○ Preheat the oven to 140°C/120°C fan/gas mark 1. Make the dead dough by spinning the flour and salt in a food processor, then cracking in the egg(s). As it's going, slowly pour in the water adding just enough that when you prod the dough it's solid, not powdery.

○ Tip it out onto a lightly floured surface and give it a quick knead, adding more flour if necessary so it's not tacky. Work it into a ball and leave on the side under a tea towel to rest.

○ Get out your chosen casseroler and do a quick check that the meat fits in it: it can be pretty squished in there as it will shrink as it cooks, but by hook or by crook it's got to get in there with the lid sitting flat (I have been known to foil-wrap a couple of bricks to call in some gravitational assistance).

○ Sit it over a high heat, pour in the oil and as it gets good and hot (but not smoking), season the leg all over with plenty of salt and pepper.

○ Seal it on the rounded outside first for a good few minutes until well browned, then repeat through all four sides over 8–10ish minutes until evenly coloured.

○ Lift out and put aside, then reduce the heat a tad. Tip in the garlic and veggies and fry for around 5 minutes whilst they soften and pick up some colour, stirring from time to time.

○ Nestle the leg back in there, then pour in the wine and when it has reduced by half, turn the heat off and add the stock along with the bay, thyme and some seasoning.

○ On a lightly floured surface, roll and stretch the dough to a sausage shape long enough to go around the entire circumference of the lid.

○ Lightly brush all around the edge of the lid and top of the pan with water to make the dough stick, then drape it around and press firmly into place, thus creating a total seal as it cooks – surprisingly satisfying. It's this total lock-in of steam and flavours that will make our beast into a beauty.

○ Pop the lid on, stick it in the oven... and come back in 7 hours: no point having a peek as there's exactly nowt to see (except the surprising juxtaposition of dough on metal), so you might as well go to the seaside or something.

○ When time's up, prise off the dough, then tuck in – the only time you'll need a knife is to get the dough off; the lamb is totally spoonable.

○ Serve up with a slew of slow-cooked garlic, some of the veggies, Alpine tatties and a judicious amount of the rich sauce – think more French jus than English gravy as the meat is plenty moist enough anyway, and along with a bit of leftover lamb, that there super-stock is the basis of a whole other world of joy in waiting...

ALPINE TATTIES

(See Austrian Tafelspitz on page 82)

(TOMORROW'S)
MOROCCAN-SPICED FREEKEH

GOOD FOR 4 OF ALL SIZES (A SURPRISING HIT WITH KIDDIES)

some of yesterday's lamb (about 200g), plus any veggies that are left over too

the lamb super-stock (ideally anywhere about 500ml)

200g freekeh

½ teaspoon ground cinnamon

½ teaspoon ground cumin

S & P

TO SERVE

2 lemons (one juice squeezed in, the other as wedges to serve)

a big handful (20g) of flat-leaf parsley, leaves picked and roughly chopped

a little Greek yogurt

sprinkling of chilli flakes (good for grown-ups, less fun for kids)

...and I'd do a green salad on the side

○ Scrape off and chuck the solidified fat, then tip the jellified stock into a measuring jug and add hot water to top up to 1 litre. Pour into a pan and bring to a simmer, then stir in the freekeh, spices and a hefty pinch of salt. Let it bubble away gently, uncovered, for 15–20 minutes, by which time all the liquid should have been absorbed.

○ Meanwhile, using a knife or your hands, roughly shred the meat and break the veg down into smaller chunks.

○ Stir it into the cooked freekeh, then squeeze in the juice of ½ lemon and seasoning to taste.

○ Eat hot or warm (or even cold the next day) with a smattering of parsley, splodges of yoggy, chilli flakes (maybe not for smalls) and more lemons on the side.

Timeline

T MINUS 8HRS
Get your lamb going

T MINUS 1HR
Spud time

NEXT DAY/ DAY AFTER
Fulfill its Freekeh risotto destiny

mutton madras

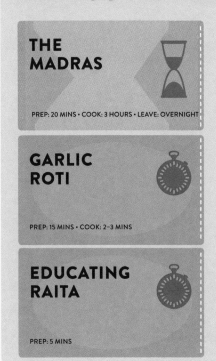

THE MADRAS

PREP: 20 MINS • COOK: 3 HOURS • LEAVE: OVERNIGHT

GARLIC ROTI

PREP: 15 MINS • COOK: 2–3 MINS

EDUCATING RAITA

PREP: 5 MINS

The rule in cooking is the older the beast, the longer it takes to become tender (though personally I seem to be getting soppier as I age), which is why mutton makes the perfect meat for this spectacular slow-cook.

You'll see the quick and easy garlic roti elsewhere in this book – they're that good and that simple, and the hopefully new-to-you raita completes this perfect triange. The first time I had dates in this cooling condiment I had a proper sit-up and take notice moment: the sweetness of this succulent desert fruit contrasted with the sharp yoggy and lime juice was arresting. 'Blimey, never seen that before' I said to myself... hence the title.

If you're a traditionalist who thinks that curry needs rice, then go for simple long-grain rice as these lot are a cacophony of full-on flavours. And whilst I see nothing wrong with a good carb, I might gently point out that what with the spuds in it and roti on the side you may want to reconsider...

Great today, better tomorrow... but the next day: bloody stratospheric.

THE MADRAS

1kg mutton, diced into 4ish cms

couple of handfuls of plain flour

40g butter

50ml plain oil, like vegetable or sunflower

3ish (500g) white onions, chopped

4 cloves of garlic, chopped

thumb-sized piece of fresh ginger (20g), unpeeled, washed, knobbly bits nicked off, finely diced

2–3 green chillies (depending on how hot you like it), split in half lengthways, seeds left in, then cut in half widthways

1 tablespoon ground turmeric

3 tablespoons madras curry powder

50g ground almonds

3 tablespoons tomato purée

400g tin chopped tomatoes

500ml chicken stock

5 bay leaves

750g potatoes, peeled and cut into rough 4cm pieces

1 green pepper, deseeded and cut into chunky pieces

4 large vine-ripened tomatoes, quartered

S & P

○ Preheat the oven to 150°C/130°C fan/gas mark 2. Put half the mutton into a colander and throw a scant handful of flour over it. Toss to coat, then season well with salt and pepper.

○ Melt half the butter in the oil in a large, wide pan over a medium–high heat. Once it's good and hot, tip the flour-dusted mutton in, turn the heat up to full and give it a quick stir. Leave for a few minutes to brown on the underside before stirring to expose a new side to the contact heat and allow to brown for a similar amount of time.

○ Meanwhile, repeat the flour and seasoning malarkey with the other half of the meat.

○ Lift the browned meat out of the pan into a bowl, chuck in the rest of the butter and, once fizzling, get the second lot going. The flour from the meat will naturally start sticking to the bottom of the pan, but if it begins to blacken in a way that smells burny, pour in a couple of tablespoons of water and use your wooden spoon to scrape it off.

○ When the second batch is browned on both sides, lift it out and put it with the first lot and then tip the onions, garlic, ginger, chillies and spices into the pan. Fry for a good 5 minutes, stirring briskly and pretty constantly, still over a high heat.

○ Plop the meat back in along with the almonds and tom purée and take the time to give it all a really good roll to coat until it looks like a happy, cohesive curry-to-be.

○ Add the tin of toms and chix stock, then lob in the bay. Give it all a good stir, taking care to scrape and incorporate all the good sticky stuff off the base of the pan. Season with salt and pepper as it comes up to a simmer, then put a lid on, stick it in the oven and walk away.

○ Have a look after 2 hours: the meat should just be showing signs of tenderising, but if it's still at the hard nugget stage, put it back in and check again in 30 minutes. Once the mutton has a bit of give to it when you squeeze a piece, stir in the spud chunks, green pepper and fresh toms then put it back in the oven for another hour, by which point the meat should be super-tender, the spuds soft and the sauce rich. And if not, just stick it back in and check again in another 30 minutes.

○ Once you're happy it's reached its moment, leave to cool, then put it away for as long as you can.

GARLIC ROTI

400g plain flour, plus extra
   for dusting

½ teaspoon salt

1–2 cloves of garlic, finely minced

2 tablespoons butter, softened

○ Tip the flour and salt into a bowl, make a well in the middle, then pour in 220ml of cold water and mix together using a wooden spoon (NB: not all the flour will be wet at this stage).

○ Turn the whole lot onto your work surface and knead for a good few minutes, at first using the excess flour from the bowl and then a few more grabs from the flour jar if necessary to stop it sticking. Your work is done when the texture is soft and smooth, like an ear lobe (for real – try it).

○ The dough is now ready to go, but if it's not needed till later, cover it with a damp cloth to stop it drying out and leave at room temp.

○ When you're ready to roti, preheat the oven to 150°C/130°C fan/gas mark 2 and lightly flour your work surface.

○ Cut the dough into six equal pieces (just over 100g each) and roll each dough ball into a thin circle, roughly 20cm diameter.

○ Put a heavy-based cast iron pan/skillet/griddle pan over a high heat and, as it's getting hot, take a minute to stir the garlic into the softened butter with a touch of salt and black pepper.

○ When your cooking device is blazing hot, lay on one floppy disc, holding it down with a spatula to stop it from bubbling up.

○ Once you get some appealing char marks on the underside (2–3 minutes) and it starts to puff up, flip it over and cook for the same amount of time on the other side.

○ Now wrap it up in a tea towel, like a present, and put in the oven to keep warm whilst you get on with the rest of them.

○ Spread each one with garlic butter, then get them to your people as quickly as you can, wrapped back up in the cloth for warmth and security.

EDUCATING RAITA

300g natural yogurt

3–4 stoned dates, chopped small

1 cucumber, peeled, deseeded and
   small diced (1–2cm sq)

2 spring onions, thinly sliced

a handful of coriander, chopped

juice of 2 limes

S & P

○ Yup, it all just gets mixed together in a small bowl then have a taste; you may need to add more lime juice as it's all about the sweet–sharp balance.

Timeline

2 DAYS/DAY BEFORE

Don't hurry the curry

AN HOUR OR SO BEFORE FEEDING TIME

Gently warm it through in the oven

Make raita (so still zippy & fresh)

Go roti, go roti (though you can make the dough ahead of time and leave it to sit if you want)

middle eastern lamb pilaf

LAMB & MERGUEZ PILAF

PREP: 20 MINS · COOK: 3 HOURS

LEBO SALAD WITH PRESERVED LEMON DRESSING

PREP: 10 MINS (PLUS 1 MONTH FOR THE LEMON!)

BEETROOT TZATZIKI

PREP: 5 MINS

The geographical span of these recipes represents pretty much my dream culinary tour: a Turkish-inspired pilaf alongside a punchy, super-fresh, Lebanesey salad with an acerbic Moroccan preserved lemon dressing, plus a Greekish tzatziki on the side.

All these mighty countries may not get on all the time (ahem) but by Jove their food does.

One, or rather three, for the texture-lovers out there: soft, biting and creamy in its parts.

LAMB & MERGUEZ PILAF

4 tablespoons olive oil

1kg diced lamb (around 4 x 4cm, if anyone's asking)

6 merguez sausages (about 300g), cut into rough 3cm pieces

2 red onions, thickly sliced

3 cloves of garlic, chopped

2 carrots, sliced

½ teaspoon ground cinnamon

½ teaspoon paprika

1 teaspoon ground cumin + ½ teaspoon seeds, ideally

1 teaspoon ground turmeric

125g dried apricots

1 litre chicken stock

300g long-grain rice

50g dried lentils (green or brown)

a big handful (20g) of flat-leaf parsley, roughly chopped

S & P

○ Preheat the oven to 150°C/130°C fan/gas mark 2. Put an ovenproof casseroler (like a Le Creuset) on the hob over a high heat with half the oil. When it's good and hot, thoroughly brown the lamb in 3–4 batches, roughly 4 minutes a time, lifting the browned meat out and setting aside, then waiting for the pan to get smoking hot again before doing the next batch.

○ Once all the lamb is done, do the same with the sausages until golden brown and set them aside too, but not with the lamb, and when they've cooled, pop them in the fridge for the time being as you don't need them for a couple of hours.

○ Throw the onions, garlic and carrots into the meaty-infused pan, reduce the heat to medium and gently fry for 5ish minutes, stirring regularly.

○ Add all the spices and stir to coat the veg for a few minutes more. Now tip the lamb plus its juices back in, along with the apricots, stock and a good amount of seasoning.

○ Stick a lid on, bring to a simmer and then put in the oven. After 2 hours, lift out and stir in the rice, lentils and merguez, then put the lid back on and put back in the oven for 45 minutes.

○ When time's up, take it out, give it a ten minute rest, taste for seasoning and serve just like that with parsley on top.

64

RAW LEBO SALAD WITH PRESERVED LEMON DRESSING

FOR THE SALAD

½ small red cabbage (300g), core cut out and thinly sliced

½ cucumber, diced

a big handful of radishes, halved

60g frozen peas, defrosted

60g sugar snap peas, sliced lengthways

a handful of mint leaves, roughly chopped

1 pomegranate, seeded

a handful of pistachios (shelled), smashed with the side of a chef's knife

a handful of dill, roughly chopped

FOR THE DRESSING

½ preserved lemon (either bought or see page 159) or 60g preserved lemon purée

2 teaspoons honey

1 clove of garlic, roughly chopped

1 teaspoon ground cinnamon

150ml olive oil

1 tablespoon white wine vinegar

juice of 1 lemon (roughly 50ml)

The dressing makes a big jarful but lasts for ages in the fridge and is a useful guy to have around – it jazzes up the simplest of leaves or try stirring it into Greek yoggy with a touch of honey as an instant crudité dip.

❍ First make the dressing by throwing all the ingredients in a blender and whizzing until smooth and creamy.

❍ Put the sliced cabbage into a bowl big enough to hold all the salad ingredients, then pour on a full ramekin/2 egg cups/75g-ish of the dressing.

❍ Give it a mix and leave to soften whilst you ready all the other components.

❍ When you're ready to go, just chuck everything in with the cabbage (but no more dressing), saving a few pom seeds, pistachios and dill fronds for the top. Toss, taste, season and serve.

Timeline

A MONTH BEFORE (!)

Make your preserved lemons (or you can buy them, but y'know... I'll never quite look at you the same way again)

3–4 HRS BEFORE LIFT-OFF

Start the pilaf (this one's better eaten on the day, after a little rest from from the oven)

ONCE IT'S IN THE OVEN

Make the p. lemon dressing (does good for a bit of sitting time)

When you've added rice and lentils to pilaff and it's back in the oven, bust out the tzatziki

Knock up and dress the salad

BEETROOT TZATZIKI (See McTurcos on page 24)

chapter three
beef

The basic principle is that the bigger the beast, the longer it takes to cook, which is why this chapter was both the easiest and the hardest to settle upon.

Easiest as there was no square-peg-into-round-holing or twisting the formula of the book to fit the ingredients: beef is big, beautiful and has a great array of cuts that take a long time to tenderise. Which is also exactly why it was the hardest... who to choose?

We narrowly miss out on the famous nose-to-tail eating by leading with its cheek (I've never cooked beef nose, so why the hell should you?). This end of our beast is in familiar territory, braised and

Bourguignon'd, but at the other end it's a different story; the tail's been given a spiced-up Caribbean makeover. Just goes to show what's traditional for some is revelationary to others.

Our journey along its length and breadth also takes in a couple of prime cuts – the nature of their marbled muscularity calls for hard and fast cooking, thus illustrating the full versatility of this mighty beast.

And having once been trodden on by one walking round a county show ring, I can attest that they really are mighty – it broke my toe!

a cheeky bourguignon

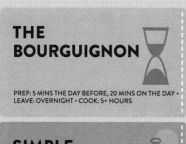

THE BOURGUIGNON

PREP: 5 MINS THE DAY BEFORE, 20 MINS ON THE DAY •
LEAVE: OVERNIGHT • COOK: 5+ HOURS

SIMPLE SMASHED SPUDS

PREP: 5 MINS • COOK: 20 MINS

PEAS & PANGRATTATO

PREP: 10 MINS • COOK: 10 MINS

I'm not sure how much cows smile, so it must be all that chewing the cud that makes their cheeks such juicy mega-nuggets of muscle, and thus a joy to cook. To really get the most out of them, marinate for a day or two before going low and slow in the oven. And this is a serious slow: it takes them a good 4–5 hours to reach their zenith, and whilst they're quietly working away in there you can be off playing elsewhere.

That famous background from the Bourgogne works just as well in this cheeky situation as with the classic dice: what's not to like about bacon, 'shrooms and lots of red wine? And after all that time alone in the pan together they really embody the phrase 'give and take'.

What emerges from the oven is so rich and deep that it would be rude not to serve it with some sauce-soaking spuds. I've circumnavigated mash in favour of some simple crushed newies, both for the reasons of promising you a Quick (and these just about qualify) and also actively preferring the texture of having the skins involved.

The other Quick serves a three-fold purpose: something green, garlicky and crunchy for sure, but also taps into our country's unanimous pleasure of peas.

THE CHEEKY BOURGUIGNON

FOR 4

1kg beef cheeks (usually 2 or 3 in number) – any decent butcher will be able to get them, and to be sure I'd order ahead

1 bottle (750ml) red wine – it's supposed to be Burgundy if you're being true to the dish, but, y'know, whatevs

3 bay leaves

10g stalks of thyme, tied together with string

2 tablespoons olive oil

120g smoked pancetta lardons

300g shallots, cut into large dice

300g chestnut mushrooms, destalked and torn in half

25g garlic, roughly chopped

2 tablespoons plain flour

500ml beef stock

S & P

○ Marinate the cheeks for a night or two in the wine, bay and thyme.

○ When you're ready to get cooking, preheat the oven to 150°C/130°C fan/gas mark 2. Drain the cheeks in a colander over a mixing bowl to catch the wine and set the bay and bunch of thyme to one side.

○ Pat the cheeks with kitchen paper so they're not dripping wet (which will cause troublesome spitting when they come into contact with hot oil) and season them lightly all over with salt and pepper.

○ Put an ovenproof casseroling pan on the hob and heat the oil in it. Chuck in the lardons and fry till golden, stirring regularly, then lift them out to drain on kitchen paper.

○ Gently lay the cheeks in the pan, rounded-side down first, and give them a good seal on both sides until they are well browned.

○ Lift them out and put with the lardons, then chuck the shallots, mushrooms, garlic + bay and thyme from the marinade into the pan.

○ Fry for a good 5–8 minutes, stirring from time to time, then once the mushrooms have started to soften, reduce the heat, give it a light seasoning and scatter in the flour.

○ Stir continuously for another couple of minutes to coat all the veggies, making sure the flour isn't sticking to the bottom of the pan and starting to burn.

○ Tip the lardons back in, give it a quick one-two with the wooden spoon, then nestle the cheeks in there too.

○ Pour in the red wine from the marinade and as it comes to a simmer, scrape the bottom of the pan with your trusty wooden spoon to dislodge any flavoursome nuggets.

○ Give it a skim if necessary, then tip in the stock, put the lid on and stick in the oven.

○ Don't even bother checking them for 4 hours – sometimes they can take up to 5. They're ready when the cheeks are super-soft and submissive to touch but still gamely holding shape.

○ Taste the background sauce for seasoning and leave to rest whilst you finish the spuds, peas and pangrattato.

SIMPLE SMASHED SPUDS

FOR 4

600g new potatoes (not too
massive – the smaller the better
as this is supposed to be a
Quick), washed or scrubbed

120ml milk

30g butter

120g crème fraîche

5ish spring onions,
thinly sliced

lots of S & P

○ Put the spuds in a saucepan, cover with cold water,
chuck in a good pinch of salt and bring to the boil
over a high heat (quicker with a lid).

○ Once at a rolling boil, take the lid off and reduce the
heat to a busy simmer until the spuds are cooked,
about 15 minutes depending on size.

○ Drain into a colander. Put the pan straight back on
the hob over a low–medium heat; pour in the milk
and melt the butter in it.

○ Tip the spuds back in and crudely smash with a
masher until broken up into chunky pieces.

○ Turn the heat off, stir through the crème fraîche and
spring onions and give it a mighty good seasoning –
this one loves both salt and pepper.

Timeline

**1 OR 2 DAYS BEFORE
NOSH-ON**

Marinate cheeks

**1 OR HALF A DAY
BEFORE**

Cook cheeks/reheat as
necessary gently
in the oven

**HALF AN HOUR
BEFORE SERVING:**

Get spuds on to boil

As they're cooking,
make pangrattato

Pea water on

Finish spuds and
cook peas

PEAS & PANGRATTATO

**PEAS FOR 4; PANGRATTATO
MAKES A SMALL BOWLFUL
OR JAM JARFUL**

200g crusty white bread with
integrity (such as sourdough
or something similar, preferably
but not essentially a day or
two old)

2–3 cloves of garlic, chopped

4 tablespoons extra virgin olive oil

zest of 2 lemons

400g frozen peas

S & P

○ For the pangrattato, cut the crusts off the bread and
tear into chunks (if it's fresh, spread out on a baking
tray and put in the oven to dry out for 5 minutes at
160°C/140°C fan/gas mark 3).

○ Load into a food processor and blitz into fine
breadcrumbs – if it's very stale you may have to stop
it once or twice to give the pieces a shuffle...and if it's
very fresh, it may not break up, so you may need to
dry the pieces in the oven a bit more, then re-blitz.

○ Once you're happy with the size of your crumbs, add
the garlic and spin again briefly.

○ Pour the oil into a wide frying pan and set it over a
medium heat. Once hot, tip in the breadcrumbs (but
don't wash up the food processor), season with salt
and pepper and fry for 5–8 minutes, stirring pretty
much all the time to get even colouration.

○ When you find yourself looking at a pan of deep
golden crunchiness, get it out of there asap to stop
it over-browning; tip back into the food processor
along with the lemon zest, give it another quick
whizz and taste for seasoning.

○ Do you really want me to tell you how to cook
the peas?!

serious steak supper

FONDANT POTATOES

PREP: 30 MINS • COOK: 1½ HOURS

GRILLED RIB-EYES

COOK: 5-9 MINS

BROWN BUTTER HOLLANDAISE

COOK: 15 MINS

Red meat, butter, carbs and more butter. If your name starts with Ella or ends with Hemsley, look away now.

But if you're a good-time girl or guy who every now and then needs to make the kind of meal that changes the complexion of your whole day, read on.

When it came to making the butter-laden fondants that I'd landed on as the perfect Slow for this recipe, I cavalierly launched myself at them as if I'd last made them yesterday. Automatic pilot kicked in as I began to slice and then trim the spuds into their characteristic lozenge shape, and it was only then that I thought back to when I last made them. Shock, horror, it had been over 20 years since that long, hot summer at The Belvedere in Holland Park, when as the lowliest chef in the kitchen consigned to the veg section, I had to shape two big buckets of them every day.

A score of years later I may not be doing much different in how I approach this old French standard, but the bit of reusing the flavour-saturated butter the potatoes cook in for the hollandaise, well, that gives me hope that the last 20 years have not been in vain... though certainly all that butter will be (in vein, that is...).

You may well want some kind of green goodness on the side, in which case for reasons of both tradition and health, watercress would be the natural choice.

FONDANT POTATOES

FOR 2, IN A GENEROUS KIND OF WAY

250g salted butter

1kg medium-sized (i.e. 150–180g each) waxy spuds, like Desiree or any that are red-skinned

few stalks of thyme or rosemary

6–8 cloves of garlic

S & P

○ Very gently melt the butter in a small pan (like your egg-boiling one) and as the white milk appears on the surface, skim it off with a spoon.

○ After about 5 minutes, when it's stopped rising, turn off the heat. There will still be some buttermilk sitting on the bottom of the pan, so very gently tip the liquid gold into a bowl, taking great care not to let any of the white stuff slip in there too (and if it does, just fish it out with a spoon), then chuck the bottom-dwelling milk away. You have just made clarified butter – congrats.

○ Now tend to your spuds, keeping in mind the lozenge shape you're heading for. Slice off about 3cm from one of the long, wide sides of your unpeeled spud and do with as you will – I'm afraid it has no part to play in this dish... blame those wasteful Frenchies. Cut the potato lengthways into ovals about 3cm thick, discarding the rounded piece on the other side too. The next step is to carefully run a little knife

METHOD CONTINUED ROUND THE BEND ...

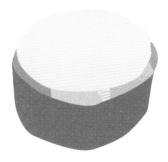

around each slice to peel off the skin (or use a peeler, but you'll still need a little knife in a min), and the last stage to make them lozenge-shaped (the traditional one for fondants) is to bevel the 90-degree corners on both sides of the spud all the way round.

○ Now choose a heavy-based frying pan (a cast iron skillet is ideal, though anything with a fat bottom works) and put the spuds in: they should be neither tightly packed nor swimming in space.

○ Pour on the clarified butter, then cold water to come three-quarters of the way up them. Dot the thyme/rosemary stalks and cloves of garlic in and around the spuds, pushing them below the surface of the liquid, then season with a good thumb-and-two-finger grab of salt and some black pepper.

○ Put the pan on the smallest burner over a medium heat, uncovered, and let it start slowly doing its thing: you want to keep it ticking over on a steady, relaxed bubble.

○ Keep a very casual eye on them for the next 45ish minutes, giving them a shuffle once or twice to stop them sticking. They're ready to turn when you stick a knife in and it meets just a bit of resistance.

○ As you turn them, change their positions in the pan (ones in the centre to the outside and vice versa) to help them cook evenly, and reduce the heat to low.

○ Give it about another 30 minutes, by which time the spuds should be cooked through and soft (check with a knife again). At this point if there's still any water left in the pan, then turn the heat up to a busy bubble to evaporate it away so you are just left with spuds frying in butter. (NB: If your spuds are super-soft and about to break, carefully lift them out and put aside until all the water has evaporated.)

○ Once there's no water left they'll start to brown and the aim is to have them golden and crunchy on both sides. Now they're going to start sticking big time, but with the right equipment (like a palette knife/metal fish slice) and a bit of patience, you should be fine to flip (though if you do lose that layer of crunchiness to the pan then no biggie, just keep frying until a new crisp underside has formed).

○ Preheat the oven to 160°C/140°C fan/gas mark 3 to keep them hot when they're ready.

○ When the spuds are pleasingly golden brown on both sides, lift them out, season with salt and keep in the oven whilst you strain the flavoursome butter through a sieve and make the Hollandaise (see opposite). Serve the confit'd garlic cloves with the spuds.

GRILLED RIB-EYES

FOR 2

2 x 250g rib-eye steaks,
at room temperature

S & P

○ Just to reiterate, the steaks must be at room temp before you start cooking them.

○ Season them well on both sides as you get a griddle or large, heavy-based frying pan searingly hot. This is a dry situation – no oil.

○ Once it's up to super-sonic temp, lay the steaks down and don't fiddle with them at all. Turn after 3 minutes for rare, and 5 minutes for medium (you can work the remainder out from there) and cook for a minute less than you did on the first side.

○ Lift off and leave to rest for 4–5 minutes before plating up.

Timeline

2-3 HOURS BEFORE STEAK TIME

Get fondants going

1 HOUR BEFORE THEY'RE READY

Steak out of fridge to come to room temp

AS SOON AS FONDANTS ARE COOKED

Strain butter, make hollandaise

Once that stress is out the way, cook the steaks

BROWN BUTTER HOLLANDAISE

MAKES A RAMEKIN-FUL
– JUST RIGHT FOR THE STEAK
AND SPUDS FOR 2

3 tablespoons white wine vinegar

1 egg yolk

the butter from the fondants (should be about 100ml), sieved and still liquid

small squeeze of lemon

¼ teaspoon salt

○ Pour the vinegar into the smallest saucepan in the house (like your egg-boiling pan), bring it slowly to a simmer and then turn the heat right down until it has reduced to just less than a teaspoon.

○ Quickly locate a small, heatproof (preferably metal), round-based bowl that sits snugly on the vinegar pan to make a double boiler. Put the egg yolk and 1 tablespoon of cold water in it and lightly whisk over the steam from the vinegar.

○ Keep whisking as the yellow mixture thickens up: it's done when the whisk leaves drag marks that last for a couple of seconds.

○ Take the bowl off the heat and slowly pour in the melted butter, whisking all the time. Finish it by pouring in the reduced vinegar.

○ Squeeze in a touch of lemon juice, season with salt (but no pepper) and stick your finger in for a greedy taste. Bloody delicious!

korean barbecue beef

BULGOGI

PREP: 5 MINS · LEAVE: OVERNIGHT · COOK: 5-10 MINS

SEOUL-FUL NOODLES

PREP: 10 MINS · COOK: 10 MINS

NON-APPROVED NUCLEAR EXPLOSION (AKA 'DOUBLE DARE PRESERVED CHILLIES')

PREP: 5 MINS · LEAVE: OVERNIGHT

Despite it being some 20 years ago that I worked in San Francisco, I continue to muddle my American and British butchery terms. In San Fran, I picked up an early-morning butcher's shift in the resto I was cheffing at just for kicks, so got in at 5am and learnt how to break down any animal, irrelevant of size, into 6oz portions by 7am.

Flank steak, as they call it in the States, or bavette, as it's mostly known here, is best when it has a bright red colour. Because it comes from a strong, well-exercised part of the cow, it is best sliced against the grain before serving, to maximise tenderness. It is frequently used in Asian cuisine, often sold in Chinese markets as 'stir-fry beef', though they're onto it in Colombia too, where it is known as 'sobrebarriga', literally meaning 'over the belly'. Also known as skirt steak, it's spot on for this dish, and becoming less of a chef's secret and more widely available (i.e. supermarkets) by the minute.

As you may gather by the slightly crass/crap titles of the Quicks, this trio of recipes comes to you courtesy of Korea, where bulgogi is a national dish, and deservedly so. Way easy, lots of fun and damned tasty, I fell in love with it in Koreatown in LA last time I was there, and in that Californian way felt the need to share it with the group (i.e. you).

BULGOGI

A FINE PARTY FOR 4

500g bavette/flank steak

FOR THE MARINADE

a bunch of spring onions, sliced into 2cm batons

5 tablespoons (75ml) dark soy sauce

2 tablespoons soft dark brown sugar

4 fat cloves of garlic, finely chopped

3 tablespoons (40g) sesame seeds, lightly toasted

3 tablespoons toasted sesame oil

lots of freshly ground black pepper (3g): about 30 twists

TO SERVE

2 heads of baby gem lettuce, leaves separated and washed

○ Slice the steak into strips about 1cm thick against the grain (this may sound technical but if you look at the piece of meat it's pretty obvious... or just ask your butcher, which is probably who you'll need to go to for this cut anyway).

○ Put the slices and three-quarters of the spring onions in a suitably snug container for their overnight stay.

○ Separately, mix together all the other ingredients for the marinade, saving a tablespoon or so of sesame seeds for laters.

○ Pour roughly two-thirds of the marinade over the steak and give it a mix so that all of the exposed surfaces are coated.

○ Cover and put in the fridge, alongside the remainder of the marinade for tomorrow.

SEOUL-FUL NOODLES

FOR 4

Timeline

DAY BEFORE
Marinate beef
Make non-approved explosion
(i.e. pickled & preserved chillies)

HALF AN HOUR BEFORE TIME
Pull beef out to come up to room temp
Prep veg
Soak noodles
Cook noodles
Grill beef

200g rice noodles (the flat ones ideally; possible with vermicelli noodles but not quite the same)

2 tablespoons toasted sesame oil

200g Chinese leaf, sliced about 2cm thick

2 carrots, shredded or grated

1 red pepper, deseeded and thinly sliced

1 tablespoon dark soy sauce

1 teaspoon fish sauce

juice of 1 lime

a big handful (10g) of mint leaves, chopped

salt, to taste

- ○ Fill then fire up the kettle; put the noodles in a heatproof bowl and cover with boiling water.

- ○ Leave for 5ish minutes until they have gone white and softened. Drain, run briefly under cold water and spread out on a tray to air-dry for a few minutes.

- ○ Heat the oil in a wide pan or wok, then chuck in the noodles, Chinese leaf, carrots and red pepper; keep the mix on the move for a few minutes so that the noodles don't stick to the bottom – my tip is to use chopsticks to stop them breaking.

- ○ Once the noodles have turned clearish again, add the soy, fish sauce, lime juice and mint and continue to stir-fry for just a minute or two.

- ○ Turn the heat off and season it up – it'll take soy and probably some salt as well, and maybe more lime juice and fish sauce to your taste.

NON-APPROVED NUCLEAR EXPLOSION
(AKA 'DOUBLE DARE PRESERVED CHILLIES')

MAKES A SMALL JAM JARFUL

10g sea salt

50ml rice wine vinegar

5 red bird's eye chillies (use standard red chillies if you want a more controlled explosion), stems cut off and sliced (seeds left in)

- ○ Put the salt and vinegar into a small jam jar, screw the lid on and shake until the salt has dissolved.

- ○ Add the chillies, making sure they are under the level of the vinegar, re-seal and leave overnight.

- ○ Shake before opening and serve just the chillies, not the liquid (beware the fire – my, how they've grown!).

THE PULL-TOGETHER

- ○ Apart from its marinade, the other defining factor of bulgogi is that it needs to be grilled. A BBQ is ideal (disposables are fun and easy), and if you have one, a bloody hot griddle over a brace of burners is also good. Failing that, go for a couple of dry frying pans – just don't overcrowd the meat and let it pick up a bit of charring.

- ○ Once your noodles are ready, warm through the marinade you kept aside and heat your chosen cooking equipment to smoking hot. Lay the meat down, being careful not to pile it up, doing it in batches if necessary.

- ○ Cook for no more than a minute or two max a side, then turn, do the same again and then get it the hell out of there.

- ○ Serve the meat with the noodles, baby gem leaves in a pile on the side and the nuclear chillies next to. Drizzle the remainder of the warmed marinade over and around the meat and noodles, then finish with the spring onions and sesame seeds you kept aside. '맛있는 피 묻은' as they say in Korea.

TAFELSPITZ

PREP: 15 MINS • COOK: 2½–3 HOURS

ALPINE TATTIES

PREP: 5 MINS • COOK: 25 MINS

TWO AUSTRIAN HORSERADISH SAUCES

PREP: 10 MINS • COOK: 5–10 MINS

austrian tafelspitz

Tafelspitz. Sounds like a word that's followed by 'Gesundheit'.

I'm guessing pretty much every country has their version of this dish... *pot-au-feu* to the French, *bollito misto* to the Italians, boiled beef to you and me and, from our Austrian friends, this new acquisition to my repertoire, the Mighty Tafelspitz.

Last New Year, Delilah-daughter and I went to Salzburg to see our old friends Mike and Jools (and I really do mean longtime buddies – Mike was my BSM driving instructor in the 80s!). Keen to glean everything I could about a cuisine I last tasted as a fifteen-year-old, I scoured restaurant menus for dishes I thought sounded interesting, but like a fool I read over the tafelspitz, thinking 'How fun can boiled beef be?' Thankfully, Mike knew better and I was green-eyed with awe when it came. The most beautiful, tender, flavoursome beef -cooked-in-stock I've ever tasted, made astronomical by the bits on the side... and we all love a bit on the side.

Crunchy spuds with onions akin to Lyonnaise but less weighty (and the slight
Scottishness in the title is a nod to Mike, who originally hailed from those parts).
And to round off this majestic meal, not one but two horseradish sauces, so different
from our now slightly dull-seeming ubiquitous creamed stuff. What a feast – truly
majestic in a way that we just don't embrace over here anymore... except maybe at
Sunday lunch or family get-togethers, which this dish is perfect for.

Back in Blighty I realised I had to include it in this book – it was the perfect Slow,
and different too from my other beef recipes as it's a stovetop one. So I got in touch
with my mates over there, who happened to be good friends with a local chef called
Ronaldo (doesn't sound very Austrian, I know, but you have to remember that part
of Austria is within [tafel-] spitting distance of the Italian border).

In a thoroughly modern way for a totally old-school dish, he sent me his family's
tafelspitz recipe over WhatsApp, and by contrast here it is in all its Hapsburgian
Old-School glory. Try it, and I guarantee you'll be as blown away as I was.

It's boiled beef, but brilliantly so, not buggered.

TAFELSPITZ

2 large onions, unpeeled and halved

1.2kg cap of rump* (ask your butcher), plus some beef bones if poss

4 carrots, topped (2 for the stock and 2 for serving)

2 medium leeks, cut in half (1 for the stock and 1 for serving)

3 sticks of celery (1 for the stock and 2 for the end)

1 tablespoon peppercorns

4 juniper berries

2 bay leaves

2 big turnips, peeled and halved/quartered, depending on size

S & P

NB: Ronaldo also says to put a few stalks of lovage in it, which adds a little something, but I can't always get hold of it.

*also known increasingly as 'picanha', as it's very popular in Brazil, and with their ex-pat community over here.

○ Choose a pan big enough to hold the meat, veg and water to cover. Put it on a medium–high heat and, once hot, lay the halved onions onto the bottom of the dry pan, cut-side down and still in their skin.

○ Sear until lightly blackened, then use a palette knife to release them and immediately pour on 3 litres water (plus the beef bones if you managed to score any). Bring to the boil, then lower in the beef and stock veg (2 carrots, 1 leek, a stick of celery and a small handful of lovage if poss). Add the peppercorns, juniper and bay, and let it settle to a steady simmer.

○ Keep the temp at a steady, slow simmer, skimming from time to time, then after 2 hours, use a slotted spoon to do a veg exchange: out with the knackered stock veg (you can leave the spices and bay), and in with the raw ones (turnips too), which will be served up with the beef. Put aside the blackened onions that are too fine and flavoursome to lose, but ditch everybody else, and submerge the new veg in the stock by resting an upturned plate directly on top of them.

○ Start checking the tafelspitz after a further 30 minutes, but it could take up to an hour: Ronaldo says, 'Doneness is recognised by a long fork/skewer entering the meat easily with no resistance.' No change there.

○ When you're happy with the tenderness, lift out the meat and veg, taste the stock.: give it a few minutes' hard boiling to reduce and intensify. Once the flavour is there, strain through a sieve and season well.

○ Put the stock, meat and veg (including the onions) back into the pan and take to the table like that (the traditional way in Österreich). Move the meat onto a board and use a long sharp knife to slice into finger-thick slabs, going against the grain of the meat so they have a strip of fat on top.

○ Serve up with the braised veg (including our fave blackened onions, still in their skin) and a couple of ladles of the stock. For the consummate Tafelspitz Experience, it really needs to be accompanied by the Alpine Tatties, both of the horseradish sauces and some buttery-nutmeg sautéed spinach too.

ALPINE TATTIES: SAUTÉED MIDS WITH ONIONS & OREGANO

1kg waxy mids potatoes (ideally red-skinned but really anything like a Ratte will do), washed and unpeeled

60ml plain oil (Ronaldo used corn oil, but I'm not fussed)

60g butter

3 white or red onions (450g), sliced

○ Preheat the oven to 180°C/160°C fan/gas mark 4. Put the spuds in a saucepan and cover with cold water, throwing a good grab of salt in there too. Stick a lid on and bring to the boil, then take the lid off and leave to simmer until the spuds are just cooked – about 15 minutes.

○ Once the spuds are rocking and rolling, put a big, heavy-based frying pan on a high heat with half the oil. Melt half the butter in it, then whilst it's fizzling but before it burns, chuck in the onions.

○ Toss/stir regularly as the onions collapse in volume and start to pick up some colour, but don't let them catch on the bottom – if they're beginning to stick, then reduce the heat to low and splash in a couple of tablespoons of cold water.

3 spring onions, sliced

3 tablespoons fresh oregano leaves,
picked and roughly chopped (if
you can't get fresh oregano, swap
for chopped fresh parsley with
1 teaspoon dried oregano)

S & P

○ Check the spuds for doneness, then drain and leave to
cool till you can handle them – I usually chuck them on
the doorstep – and slice into rough 3cm discs.

○ Once the onions are golden all over, tip them into a
sieve sitting over a bowl and give the pan a quick wipe
out with kitchen paper.

○ Pour the excess onion oil back into the pan with the
remainder of the oil and butter and put over a high heat.

○ When the butter is beginning to brown, chuck in the
spud slices – you may have to do this in two batches,
depending on the size of your pan. Sauté hard and fast,
giving them the odd toss along the way until they're
crisping on the outside, then stir in the sautéed onions.

○ Season with gusto (and gustissimo with the black
pepper) and toss with the spring onions and oregano.

 ## APFELKREN (THE APPLEY ONE)

80g fresh horseradish, peeled and
grated on the small holes (or
freshly grated from a jar)

4 sweet-sour apples (Royal Gala
are ideal), peeled, cored and
grated on the big holes

20g chives, finely chopped

juice of ½ lemon (depending on
how sweet the apples are)

S & P

○ Grate the horseradish a good hour before you're
planning to eat, but only grate the apples at the last
minute as they lose both crunch and colour.

○ When the time has come, stir together the grated
apples, horseradish and chives, then taste and season
with the lemon juice, salt and pepper.

 ## SEMMELKREN (THE BREADY ONE)

70g fresh horseradish, peeled and
grated on the small holes (or
freshly grated from a jar)

500ml whole milk

250g bread with crusts, preferably
a bit stale

about 300ml beef stock from
the pot

lots of S & P

○ Infuse the horseradish into the milk in a pan over a
low–medium heat for a good 5 minutes.

○ Tear the bread into chunks and throw it in there. Allow
to soften and soak for a few minutes, then tip the whole
lot into a blender and whizz briefly till smooth – it
needs to be totally lump-free, but don't leave it spinning
any longer than necessary as you'll get the gluten in the
bread going, which makes it a bit pasty.

○ Pour back into the pan, ladle in the reduced stock, which
enhances both the look and flavour (I've always been a
fan of beige), and season it up to the hilt. Have a taste,
stirring in a bit more of the yum beef stock/seasoning if
you fancy. Serve warm, in the pan, with a ladle.

Timeline

**AROUND 4
HOURS
BEFORE
SERVING**

Get your
Tafel on

**ANY TIME YOU
FEEL LIKE IT**

Make the
semmelkren
up to the
point where
the stock is
added

1HR BEFORE

Get tatties on

Grate & macerate
horseradish for
Apfelkren

Start frying onions
then spuds

**ONCE BEEF IS
READY**

Add stock to
semmelkren
and season

Grate apples
and finish
Apfelkren

jamaican oxtail stew

jamaican oxtail stew

DANDAN'S JAMAICAN OXTAIL STEW

PREP: 40 MINS • COOK: 4ISH HOURS • LEAVE: OVERNIGHT IF POSS

SALT & SWEET PLANTAIN

PREP: 5 MINS • COOK: 5–10 MINS

FESTIVALS

PREP: 10 MINS • COOK : 20 MINS

I love oxtail but was getting a little over the familiar, traditional Brit method, then my best buddy Danny introduced me to the Jamaican way... and what a revelation!! So much more interesting and multi-levelled with its firm but gentle spicing and surprisingly yummy accompaniments.

The plantains need to look well blackened (like a banana does when you start thinking about having to make banana bread, again), be a bit squidgy when you squeeze them and peel easily if you tug at the tops, or else they'll taste like cardboard instead of sweet and starchy. You're best off buying them from an Afro-Caribbean shop or street market (as opposed to a farmers' market where I don't think you'll have much luck for reasons of climate and culture). You can get them pristine, yellow and hard as nails from supermarkets, then ripen at home, but in my experience they're never as good as the battered-looking ones, and are more expensive too.

And then to the gloriously named Festivals: basically a sausage-shaped doughnut. As naughty as fried bread and as satisfying as a dumpling, these truly do take our oxtail into a full-on carnival.

NB: If you're doing the work the day before – a good idea in terms of flavour harmony – stop just before the okra goes in, then the next day lay them on top of the cold meat, tightly foil again and reheat for an hour at 160°C/140°C fan/gas mark 3.

P.S. DanDan's boy, Benjy, likes it with salad cream – a popular condiment over in those gorgeous islands.

I was sceptical but it bloody works!

DANDAN'S JAMAICAN OXTAIL STEW

Timeline

2kg oxtail, in various sizes of vertebrae pieces – not a whole tail!

FOR THE SPICE MIX

1 teaspoon ground allspice

½ teaspoon ground nutmeg

½ teaspoon ground ginger

½ teaspoon ground cloves

½ teaspoon black pepper (ground not corns)

2 teaspoons salt

FOR THE VEG SECTION

2 tablespoons vegetable oil

750g white onions, chopped

250g carrots, quartered lengthways, then sliced into small dice

1 Scotch bonnet, deseeded and diced (wash hands well after and be careful what you touch, if you know what I mean)

20g garlic, chopped

2 red peppers, deseeded and cut into small dice

1 teaspoon chilli flakes

15g thyme stalks, tied together with string

4 bay leaves

S & P

TO COMPLETE THE STEW

2 tablespoons tomato purée

1 litre beef stock

2 x 400g tins butter beans, drained and rinsed

300g okra, tops off and tails nipped

salad cream, to serve

○ Preheat the oven to full whack, about 240°C/220°C fan/gas mark 9. Stir everybody in the spice mix with the salt in a large bowl.

○ Toss the oxtail pieces into the bowl and coat well, then arrange them in a large roasting tray so that the big ones are round the outside and the little guys are in the middle. You want them to be standing on end and not touching.

○ Stick in the oven for 30–40 minutes, rotating the tray halfway through, until they are well browned and sealed.

○ Once the oxtail is in, get cracking on the veg section. Heat the oil in a wide pan over a medium–high heat. Add everything in the veg section, season and give it a shuffle every now and then as it softens, about 10ish minutes.

○ Dollop in the tomato purée, stir well and then once everything is nicely coated, pour in the stock plus 1 litre water. Bring to a simmer, then turn the heat off.

○ Once the oxtail is ready, take the tray out of the oven and reduce the temperature to 120°C/100°C fan/gas mark ½.

○ Carefully tip out all the fat, then stand the pieces back on end and pour the contents of the pan over them, taking care that the veggies are submerged and not sitting on top of the meat.

○ Cover tightly with foil and put on the middle shelf of the oven. After 2½ hours, turn them over, stir in the butter beans, re-foil as before and pop it back in. After another hour, if you're eating oxtail today, lift the foil, scatter the okra on top, cover tightly again and put it back in for a final 45 minutes. If it's for tomorrow then leave to cool with foil on and store somewhere cold overnight before following the instructions in the intro.

○ Once all is said and done, take it out and leave to chill out (as is the Jamaican way)for a good 10-ish mins with the foil on to let the flavours settle down in there.

Timeline

A DAY OR TWO BEFORE OX-NOSHING

Cook up to the point where okra goes in

AN HOUR AND 15 BEFORE OX-NOSHING

Preheat oven

AN HOUR BEFORE OX-NOSHING

Oxtail in with okra (foiled)

Make festival dough and shape

Cook plantains and put in oven

Then fry festivals... and Soul Shake Down party!

SALT & SWEET PLANTAIN

plain oil (such as vegetable or corn), for frying (same one as for cooking the Festivals)

4 plantain, peeled and cut into 2cm slices on a bit of an angle

2 tablespoons caster sugar

1 teaspoon salt

○ Preheat the oven to 160°C/140°C fan/gas mark 3.

○ Now there are two ways you can go about cooking these: either you can deep-fry them in the same pan of oil as the festivals (in which case do them first and keep warm in the oven), or shallow–fry them in a frying pan. Option one is way less effort – just chuck them in and cook for about 5 minutes, stirring occasionally – and definitely gets the job done fine, but to me you just do get a better result if you go down the frying pan route, which goes like this...

○ Put a wide frying pan over a medium heat and ladle in enough oil to cover the bottom of the pan to a depth of 1cm.

○ When the oil is hot but nowhere near smoking, put the first batch of plantain slices in so that they are closely-packed but in a single layer.

○ Shallow-fry them over a medium heat until golden and beginning to brown on the underside, reducing the heat if they're darkening too much (they'll take between 5–8 minutes, depending on how ripe they were to start with), then turn them over and cook for a little less time on the other side.

○ When you clock them turning a smashing orangey colour and they are soft when prodded in the middle, lift them out and drain briefly on kitchen paper.

○ Mix together the sugar and salt, then sprinkle generously all over. Stick them in the oven to keep warm and get on with the next lot.

FESTIVALS

FOR THE DOUGH

330g plain flour

60g fine cornmeal

³/₄ teaspoon salt

3 tablespoons caster sugar

2 teaspoons baking powder

1¹/₂ teaspoons vanilla extract

TO COOK AND FINISH

1 litre vegetable oil, for frying

2 tablespoons caster sugar

1 teaspoon salt

○ Put the dry ingredients for the dough into a mixing bowl, stir briefly and then make a well in the middle. Pour in about 200ml water along with the vanilla extract and stir with a wooden spoon to roughly bring it together.

○ Tip onto a work surface then knead, incorporating the dry flour as you go until you have a smooth dough – just a couple of minutes all in.

○ Divide it into six equal pieces and with the palms of your hands roll each one out into a sizeable fat sausage, about 20cm long. Ideally, you don't want it to be smooth on the outside but a bit ridgey, gnarly and rugged – those crevices and creases crisp up something lovely when fried.

○ Heat the oil in a suitably wide, deep saucepan to a depth of about 3cm. It needs to be hot but not stupidly so (about 160°C if you happen to have a kitchen thermometer), as the dough needs time to cook through without the outside going too dark – it's ready when you lower one in and it fizzles and floats... but not in a crazy way.

○ Fry 2–3 at a time, depending on the size of your pan (they'll puff up a bit as they cook), for around 10 minutes, turning and basting them regularly so that they colour evenly, until they're golden all over. Whilst they're getting glorious in there, line a tray with kitchen paper as a landing mat.

○ As the festivals are frying, mix together the sugar and salt to finish – the same mix as for the plantains.

○ Once the festivals are good to go, lift out with a slotted spoon, give them a quick degrease on the kitchen paper, then shifty them onto an ovenproof dish and sprinkle generously with the salt–sugar mix.

○ Keep them warm in the oven (which should already be on for your plantain) whilst you cook the remainder of them, then get thee to thine oxtail.

chapter four

pork

Pigs are where it's at. They hold a place dear to my heart not only for their fabulous wares, but strange as it may sound, in our family we have always related to them in an emotional way. My daughter's nickname (well, one of them) is Piggling or Small Pork, just as mine was in turn as a youngster. I am now Mama Pig, our cat is Lily-pig and unsurprisingly, our guinea pig is just plain Piggy. On my signet ring I have a fat little piglet that my sister Floss drew and then had engraved for my eighteenth birthday, and the next generation of cousins seem well up for continuing the tradition: instead of shouting goodbye to each other down the street, they all erupt in a belting chorus of 'PIGS!' as the family sign-off.

It's a pig thing, and you either get it or you don't.

One thing a lot of folks don't realise about pigs is that legislation still allows them to be kept in a completely intensive confinement i.e. never going outside, being kept in pens with nothing to do and suffering routine mutilations without anaesthetic, like tail docking and teeth clipping. Ouch. Not only is it inhumane, barbaric and morally wrong, but on a more base level also renders tasteless meat: pigs are now bred to fatten fast, growing quicker than nature ever intended, without any opportunity to trot around and develop muscles.

So please, look on the label and ideally only buy pork that says 'free-range' or 'organic'; 'outdoor reared' is a bit misleading as it only applies to the first 20 weeks of their lives, but it's a vast improvement on no outside time at all. Take the time and pennies to make this choice, not only for the pig's sake but for both your palate and peace of mind too.

The near worshipful status they hold for me carries through to the kitchen: adoration and respect is how I approach any pig-led cook... tripled with a borderline unhealthy amount of desire.

But in a perfect world, isn't that exactly how all kitchen adventures should begin?

porky pancetta ragù

THE RAGÙ WITH PAPPARDELLE

PREP: 20 MINS • COOK: 3 HOURS • LEAVE: OVERNIGHT

PANGRATTATO

PREP: 5 MINS • COOK: 5–10 MINS

BLITZED KALE SALAD WITH ANCHOVY & LEMON

PREP: 10 MINS

This qualifies as a seriously slow Slow – or rather part-stationary – as although the ragù only takes a few hours to cook, it is SO much better if it sits overnight (or as a minimum cools completely) before being reheated and tossed through the pasta.

The kale salad on the side is a bit of a curve ball; when I eat a deep, slow-cooked ragù like this one (on average once a fortnight from October till Feb), I need something raw and fresh either before, during or after. Simple lettuce leaves just can't stand up to the powerful pork, and anyway, nature tells us we should be eating more robust greens at that time of year. It's true that in other places in this book I've made fun of the kale-sayers, but in truth I really do like the taste as well as what it does for you... and I'm not ashamed to say so. As Kermit so sagaciously points out, 'It's not easy being green'.

The rest of this salad is a rather-too-close-for-comfort take on a signature dish of one of my top NYC chefs, Jonathon Waxman. I go to Barbuto on Washington and Twelfth every time I'm there to soothe my craving. Best roast chicken too.

Anyway, this is mine, but his is better, so do go and try it if you're over there.

Pasta is a fine supporting mechanism for this rich dish of slow-cooked Italian porkiness; it's accessible, quick and easy. But in my dream world I'd actually eat this with risotto Milanese, that is to say an understated saffrony one. There's something about the soft on soft that's evocatively rude when you put it in your mouth.

THE RAGÙ WITH PAPARDELLE

THE RAGÙ MAKES ABOUT 6 PORTIONS, BUT SHE FREEZES BEAUTIFULLY IF THAT'S MORE THAN YOU HAVE/NEED TO FEED...

2 tablespoons olive oil

250g unsmoked pancetta lardons

1kg diced pork shoulder

2 carrots, chunkily sliced

2 red onions, halved

2 sticks of celery, sliced

7 cloves of garlic, peeled but left whole

½ teaspoon chilli flakes

1 teaspoon fennel seeds

a big handful (20g) of flat-leaf parsley, leaves picked and chopped

2 bay leaves

½ teaspoon dried oregano

3 tablespoons tomato purée

200ml white wine

400g tin chopped plum tomatoes

500ml chix stock

S & P

TO SERVE

splash of olive oil

75g pappardelle per person (i.e. 300g for 4; 450g for 6)

15g basil, leaves picked and roughly chopped

about 30g nugget of Parmesan, finely grated

○ Preheat the oven to 160°C/140°C fan/gas mark 3 and reach for your favourite ovenproof casseroler.

○ Sit it over a medium heat on the hob, then pour in the oil and when it's good and hot, then tip in the pancetta. Stir for a few minutes as the fat melts and the piggy nuggets turn golden, then lift out onto kitchen paper.

○ Crank the heat up, season the diced pork with salt and pepper, then tip into the smoking oil; depending on the pig, it'll take anywhere from 10–15ish minutes for all the liquid to come out of it and reduce away, leaving you with just oil in the bottom of the pan. Only now can the meat actually start the sealing stage, creating caramelisation on the flesh, which all adds to the bonzo flavour at the end.

○ Whilst this is all going on, put the carrots in a food processor and pulse into small pieces, then add the onions, celery and garlic and pulse again until it's all of a similar size – do not purée to mush.

○ Once the pig is nicely browned, lift it out with a slotted spoon, put with the lardons and then tip the veg, chilli flakes, fennel seeds, parsley, bay and oregano into the pan.

○ Fry, stirring from time to time, for about 6–8 minutes until the veg begins to soften, then reintroduce both the pig bits to the pan, squirt in the tom purée and give it all a really thorough roll around so everything is well coated.

○ Keep stirring for just a couple of minutes, then pour in the wine, which will fairly quickly reduce and be absorbed.

○ Tip in the tin of toms and the chicken stock; season lightly with salt and a bit more heavily with black pepper as you bring it all to a simmer.

○ Pop it in the oven with the lid on: it'll be ready in 2½ –3 hours, and if you happen to be passing any time roughly halfway through, then you might as well give it a stir, but that's more for interest/security than actually doing anything useful to the end product. If you do opt for the half-time shifty, then don't worry if you think it looks a bit oily – all that great flavour will get sucked in over the second leg of the cooking (which makes my taste buds excited and my aorta sigh).

○ The ragù is ready when the pork is tender to the point of breaking up when you squish it. Now leave it to cool completely – I usually stick it on my doorstep overnight... and any intrepid urban fox tempted to approach can beware a scalded nose.

○ When you're up for eating, put a big pan of water on for the pasta with a splash of oil and some salt, and once at a rolling boil, drop the pappardelle in and stir immediately.

○ Meanwhile, gently heat the ragù on the stove and warm a big serving dish and shallow serving bowls in a low oven.

- When the pasta is cooked, drain it, but keep a cupful of the water. Immediately give the ribbons a quick fluff with a fork so it doesn't all stick together.

- Put the pasta back into the pan it was cooked in (no heat under it), ladle in the hot ragù and if it looks a bit sticky or oily (it might look both or neither), then glug in about a third of the saved pasta water at a time until you're happy with the look and consistency.

- Use tongs to move it all over to the serving dish, scatter on the basil and some Parmesan (but don't go over-kill on the cheese), and if you have any truly great extra virgin knocking around, then personally I'd crown it with a handsome splash of liquid gold.

PANGRATTATO (See Cheeky Bourguignon on page 71)

BLITZED KALE WITH ANCHOVY & LEMON

FOR 6 AS A SIDE TO THE RAGÙ

250g kale (the supermarket kind that's already off the stalk – if you're getting it from the market, then go for more like 350g)

3 tablespoons extra virgin olive oil

½ quantity of Pangrattato (see page 71)

6 anchovy fillets, finely chopped

20g Parmesan, finely grated

juice of ½–1 lemon, to taste

plenty of freshly ground black pepper… and potentially a little bit of salt, depending on how high you like your seasoning

- If necessary strip the kale leaves from their stalks, then put the leaves in a food processor (stalks go to the guinea pigs).

- Pulse till blitzed into little pieces, then tip into a bowl, pour in the oil and black pepper and rub it in between the flats of your palms for a minute or less. This is the infamous 'kale massaging' and does two things: makes the kale a brighter green as it releases the chlorophyll and gets rid of some of the bitterness (supposedly).

- The final toss together needs to be last minute to keep the breadcrumbs crunchy; when you're ready to serve, just chuck everything else in with the kale, saving a couple of tablespoons of the Pangrattato for the top.

- Mix well, taste for seasoning (lemon juice, black pepper and maybe a touch of salt) and serve with a final scattering of the crunchy breadcrumbs… at which point you may notice more than a passing resemblance to Chinese crispy seaweed.

Timeline

A DAY BEFORE YOU NEED TO EAT/ON THE DAY IF NEEDS BE

Pig your life up (as in make the ragù)

AN HOUR OR SO BEFORE PIG 'N' PASTA TIME

Make the pangrattato

Put the pasta water on

Next make the rest of the kale salad (keeping the crunchy breadcrumbs separate)

(Once the water is boiling, cook pasta)

Mix breadcrumbs into salad

Join ragù with pasta and finish

THE BELLY

PREP: 5 MINS • LEAVE: OVERNIGHT
(OPTIONAL) • COOK: 4 HOURS

PECAN COLESLAW

PREP: 10 MINS

SCOOBY SARNIE

PREP: 10 MINS

szechuan treacle crusted belly

Once upon a time there was a restaurant called Blackfoot that I had a part in. The food part, unsurprisingly. For most of its two-year life it was happy and full of laughter, but it wasn't very good at making Real Money and was increasingly rather needy time-wise (as all restaurants are), and in the end we pulled the plug and our baby slid down the hole.

This really special belly was our best seller, and the recipe I was proudest of on the menu. When we did it in the resto we used a cold-smoked belly (hence why it was on the menu as 'The Long Smoke'), but really it tastes just as good without, and in truth it's all about that killer crust. Szechuan and black peppercorns, star anise and black treacle. It's deep, intense, memorable and totally does the business when parked up against the cooling pecan slaw (a happy kitchen accident after a drunken night out: tub of dirty slaw in the fridge, pack of pecans on the table; and the rest, as they say, is history).

THE BELLY

1.6–1.8kg hunk of pork belly, off the bone and skin off

FOR THE BRINE (OPTIONAL)

2 litres water

500ml cider vinegar (more than one average supermarket bottle) 300g rock salt

170g soft brown sugar

2 onions, peeled and very roughly chopped

2 sticks of celery, washed

2 carrots, sliced

3 bay leaves

1 tablespoon peppercorns

2 pieces star anise

FOR THE CRUST

20g Szechuan peppercorns

60g black peppercorns

6 star anise

1/2 teaspoon cloves

80g black treacle

50g honey

70g soft dark brown sugar

100ml cider vinegar

1 teaspoon sea salt

You don't have to brine but it does make it tastier, more tender and keeps the meat pleasantly pinky too (as opposed to grey, which is the usual colour of slow-cooked pork).

○ So, if you're brining, bring everything to the boil, then cool completely before lowering the meat into it and leaving it to do its thing overnight.

○ Next day, (or now, if you are skipping the brining), start by making the crust. In a blender/spice grinder/coffee grinder, whizz both kinds of peppercorns with the star anise and cloves to a textured powder (i.e. still some bits in there).

○ Gently heat the black treacle, honey, sugar and vinegar in a small saucepan, give it a quick whisk to bring it together, then stir in the blitzed spices and salt. Keeping the heat low, let it gently simmer and reduce for about 10 minutes, stirring from time to time, until it's deep, rich and about 250–300ml in volume, at which point it will be almost tar-like in look and feel. Leave to cool to room temp to thicken up.

○ Preheat the oven to 140°C/120°C fan/gas mark 1 and find a roasting tray or dish that will hold the pork pretty snugly. Line it with parchment paper, so that it comes up the sides too (it gets a bit sticky as it cooks so this really helps with the washing up later).

○ Lift the belly out of the brine (whose job is now done, so it's sink 'n' bin bound), pat to dry it well, then put it in its cooking vessel and use a spoon to totally coat the meat in the glaze on all sides, encouraging it to pool on top. Slow roast, uncovered, in the oven for 4 hours, by which point the meat will be super-soft and the glaze will have turned into a fabulously textured crust.

○ Take it out and give it a decent 10-minute rest in the cool air of the kitchen for the crust to firm up, then move the meat onto a chopping board. Carefully lift up the parchment paper and tip/scrape any goodness sitting in there into a small bowl (but try and avoid all the fat), then spoon this over the meat. Find yourself a long, sharp knife and cut into long slices. Boom-shakka-lakka-boom!

IF YOU LIKE IT HOT, AND SOME DO, THEN THIS IS REALLY GOOD WITH THE NON-APPROVED NUCLEAR EXPLOSION (AKA 'DOUBLE DARE PRESERVED CHILLIES') ON THE SIDE – SEE PAGE 79.

PECAN COLESLAW

300g red cabbage, shredded into
1cm-thick slices

300g white cabbage, shredded into
1cm-thick slices

200g carrots (about 3), grated on
the big holes

10g sea salt

10g caster sugar

2 tablespoons cider vinegar

1 banana shallot, diced

a small handful (10g) of flat-leaf
parsley, chopped

2 handfuls (80g) of pecans, very
roughly chopped

2 handfuls (40g) of pumpkin seeds

70g salad cream

40g mayonnaise

extra S & some P

○ In a bloody big bowl, mix both cabbages with the carrots.

○ Chuck in the salt, sugar and vinegar, then briefly massage it into
the strands to give it a quick macerate whilst you weigh out all the
remaining ingredients.

○ Mix everything together and season to taste. The smart cook with an
eye on the Scooby Sarnie would put aside a little bowlful now as it
tends to all disappear once it's on the table.

Timeline

DAY BEFORE

Brine pork

ON THE DAY

Make crust >> slow
roast belly

**ANY TIME ON
THE DAY, UP TO
THE TIME THE BELLY
COMES OUT**

Macerate and make
coleslaw

NEXT DAY

Scooby sarnie!

SCOOBY SARNIE

a couple of slices of bread with structure (i.e. not prone to disintegrate – you need all the help you can get to keep this Mofo together; sourdough is ideal) or a small baguette

bit of mayonnaise (just for a tad more fat) – try Kewpie Japanese mayo if you ever come across it, but nowt wrong with good ole Hellmann's

thick slice of the cooked pork belly, plus crust, heated in the oven or under the grill

small bowl of the slaw

dill pickles, sliced

slice of good, strong, nutty cheese (Comté, Gruyère, mature Cheddar, Emmenthal, etc), laid on top of the pork in the oven/grill to melt

... and I dare you to squeeze some Doritos in there too...

○ I'm not really going to tell you how to make this, but I will give you one piece of advice: once your build is done, realise that for the next 10 minutes you will be committed to a monogamous relationship. Do not attempt to read a book/look at your phone/itch your nose/answer the door/communicate in any meaningful way. I tried; it just doesn't work... but my, when it's good, how sweet is that one-on-one feeling?

burgers with bacon jam

SMOKEY BACON JAM

PREP: 10 MINS • COOK: 1 HOUR

SPANISHY PORK BURGERS

PREP: 10 MINS • COOK: 10–15 MINS

QUINCE AIOLI

PREP: 5 MINS

This may just be the best pork burger ever. I say that not in a smart-ass way, as all of the components came *to* me, as opposed to *from* me. The bit of mixing pork mince with black pudding was from a brunch hash we had on the menu at my ex-Piggy restaurant, Blackfoot, and was the brainchild of the very talented James Knight, our Head Chef there (it came with a fried egg and a little light meat juice... ok, a jus).

He also brought the quince aioli to that menu, where it was served with our Iberico burger, but said he'd nicked it from his old bosses and my old friends Sam and Sam Clark at Moro.

And the bacon jam was the work of my fine co-cook on this book, Deniz Safa, who makes the best bacon jam of any Muslim I've ever met. It's surprisingly and conveniently spreadable straight from the fridge – try it on a piece of toast with scrambled eggs for a weekend hangover brekkie. Only trouble was, at the ideas stage of this book, we envisaged the bacon jam to be the Slow... and in fact it turned out to be more of a Medium (1 hour start to finish), but by this point we'd made the threesome, and together they were too good to throw out of the book. Hey-ho, and hopefully you'll forgive me once you've tried them.

Anyway, all I did was put the three components all together in a soft roll (not a burger bun, please) and reap the rewards of their combined extraordinary marvellousness.

SMOKEY BACON JAM

MAKES A BIG JAM JARFUL (MORE THAN YOU NEED FOR THE BURGERS, BUT IT LASTS FOR A COUPLE OF WEEKS IN THE FRIDGE, AND YOU'LL NEVER REGRET HAVING IT THERE)

2 tablespoons olive oil

1 red onion, finely diced

12 cloves of garlic, finely chopped

250g diced smoked pancetta (available in most supermarkets)

½ teaspoon smoked paprika

110g dark soft brown sugar

50ml maple syrup

100ml cider vinegar

S & P

○ Heat the oil in a medium-sized saucepan and gently fry the onion and garlic without browning until soft and sweet, roughly 8ish minutes.

○ Still on a low heat, add the pancetta and keep frying gently until all the fat comes out of it, roughly 10–15 minutes.

○ Increase the heat a tad and stir as the pancetta turns a dark golden colour and begins to stick to the bottom of the pan, then sprinkle in the paprika and give it all a good roll and coat.

○ Add all the remaining ingredients along with 4 tablespoons water, bring to a simmer, then turn down a bit and let it bubble away gently for 20–25 minutes until the liquid has reduced to a thick and sticky binding syrup.

○ Leave to cool for 5 minutes, then tip into a food processor and blitz to a chunky purée. This is best at room temp but also good straight from the fridge.

QUINCE AIOLI

100g quince paste or membrillo
(available from pretty much any
deli/cheese shop)

1 clove of garlic, finely chopped

2 tablespoons white wine vinegar

1 tablespoon warm water

160ml oil (ideally half plain olive
and half extra virgin, but 50:50
extra virgin and sunflower oil
also works)

S & P

○ Put the quince paste, garlic and vinegar in a
food processor with the warm water and a
couple of decent pinches of salt.

○ Whizz it for a minute before slowly adding the
oils in a thin stream (with the processor still
running, natch).

○ Once it's all incorporated, go in handsomely
with the pepper mill, then give it a final taste
for seasoning.

Timeline

**A DAY OR
TWO BEFORE**

You can make the
bacon jam on the day or
2/3/4 etc days before

**WHEN YOU'RE HALF
AN HOUR-ISH FROM
WANTING BURGERS**

First mix and shape the
burgers, then leave to
rest in the fridge
whilst you make the
quince aioli

Finally, cook the
burgers and build

SPANISHY PORK BURGERS

FOR THE BURGERS

600g pork mince

120g black pudding, roughly
chopped or crumbled, depending
on what kind you get

1½ teaspoons salt

good few twists of black pepper

FOR THE BUILD

the cooked burgers

4 burger-sized slices of
Manchego cheese

4 decent white rolls (not
burger buns)

some Smokey Bacon Jam
(see opposite)

some Quince Aioli (see above)

a couple of handfuls of rocket

○ Put all the ingredients for the burgers into a mixing bowl and really
scrunch them together well – this is easiest done with your hands, and
you can latex or not as you choose.

○ Shape into four burgers, then squish the middle a bit on each side to
make the centres thinner than the outsides (see 'Why the Dimple?' on
page 25 if you're wondering why).

○ Heat a griddle and once it's properly hot, lay the burgers on. If you don't
have a griddle, you can either cook them in a heavy-based dry frying
pan (like a skillet) or do them under the grill. Cook for about 5 minutes,
then gently try to lift one (unless you're doing them under the grill, in
which case just go ahead and turn them): if it comes away it's ready
to be turned, and if it sticks it needs a bit more time, so try again in
another minute or so, reducing the heat if they're getting too charred.

○ Once they've had about the same amount of time on the other side,
reduce the heat if you haven't done so already and put the slices of
Manchego on top of them to melt. If you're doing it on the stove top,
the top tip on getting the cheese to melt quickly is to tip a tablespoon
of water into the space between the burgers (not on them), then cover
the whole thing immediately with a big bowl. Repeat with another
tablespoon of water a minute or so later, replacing the bowl afterwards
– the steam created speeds things up nicely.

○ Check they're cooked by either sticking a skewer in and seeing if it
comes out hot, or just gently break one open and have a peek.

○ When you're happy that the burgers are ready, load up the rolls with
bacon jam on one side and quince aioli on the other. Slip the cheese-
topped burgers in there, top with some rocket and... you know what's
good for you.

pork shoulder, prunes & pie

SORT-OF-SLOW SHOULDER WITH PRUNES & PERRY

PREP: 10 MINS • COOK: 1½–2 HOURS

TURNIP ROSTI

PREP: 10 MINS • COOK: 20 MINS

A DIFFERENT KIND OF PORK PIE

PREP: 20 MINS • COOK: 30–40 MINS

This shoulder is a definite contender for least-effort-yielding best result. It's a proper pop-it-in-the-oven-and-walk-away number, but without meaning to question a fair number of recipes in this book, whilst always delivering on flavour, that technique can sometimes lack finesse. Not this baby: rich, porky, pruney goodness in a way that goes down well at both family suppers and with grown-up guests.

It's not the slowest slow-cook in the book: in fact at just under the 2-hour mark it really only just squeals into that category, but something funny happened with this trio of recipes and if I'm being totally honest, neither of the quicks quite hit my prescribed definition of 20 minutes or less. More like 30+ minutes for the rosti that just rocks with the flavours in the roasting tray (turnips and prunes... ask any Frenchie), and the Different Kind of Pork Pie, well, if you really get your skates on I reckon you can make it in 20 minutes, but then it takes another 30ish minutes in the oven... see what I mean? It's like the firm Quick Quick Slow principle went out the window and this threesome went through a bit of a mangled time warp... and now all the gents are wearing suspenders.

Nothing wrong with that though, and just to bring it back home, these really are one of my top trios in the book. You'll probably want some kind of veg action on the side: my very talented chef friend Frances, who tested this for me, did it with cabbage and carrots, which I think sounds about spot on.

By the way, using perry was an accident – that's what happens when you send a Turk out to buy cider – but it worked like a dream. Good with cider too, but I kind of like the idea of helping to keep those pear farmers in business.

SORT-OF-SLOW SHOULDER
WITH PRUNES & PERRY

1.8kg (ish) joint of pork shoulder,
  boned and rolled (fresh please,
  not from the freezer, otherwise
  that would be a frozen shoulder
  and that's not good)

oil, for brushing

2 onions, halved

1 fat or 2 small carrots, halved

200g prunes, stoned weight

3 bay leaves

1.5 litres perry or medium-dry
  cider

S & P

○ Preheat the oven to 240°C/220°C fan/gas mark 9. Get out your favourite roasting tray and sit the pork in it. Brush the skin lightly with whatever oil you have to hand, season well all over, then surround it with the onions, carrot, prunes and bay.

○ Pour the perry/cider over the onions, not over the meat, and once the oven is up to speed, put it in on the middle shelf.

○ After 45 minutes, turn the oven down to 190°C/170°C fan/gas mark 5 and take the tray out, leaving the door open to cool the oven down whilst you give both the pork and the veggies a quick baste with the juices in the bottom of the pan.

○ Put it back in the oven and, after another 45 minutes, take it out and check it's cooked by sticking a skewer into the very middle of it, leaving it there for a count of five, then gingerly putting it to your top lip. If it's cold or tepid, put it back and check again in another 15 minutes, and if it's hot enough to startle you, then it's overcooked already – sorry. The ideal temp lies exactly in the place between the two.

○ Move the pig and all the bits around it onto a warmed serving dish, cover loosely with foil and put aside for a 10-minute rest.

○ Whilst the joint is chillin' out, put the roasting tray with the cooking liquor on the hob to reduce; taste as it intensifies in flavour – I think it's about right when it's down to just a couple of centimetres deep in the bottom of the tray (the shy side of 500ml).

○ It's almost wrong that something this good requires so little effort... or maybe that's just my overeager work ethic talking.

S

L

O

W

TURNIP ROSTI

600g spuds, peeled (the perceived wisdom is that waxy spuds make a better rosti, but I've always preferred floury ones)

400g turnips, peeled

couple of sprigs of rosemary, leaves picked and finely chopped

2 tablespoons animal fat (i.e. duck/pig/butter)

S & P

○ Preheat the oven to 220°C/200°C fan/gas mark 7. Grate the spuds and turnips, then mix them together in a bowl. Grab a biggish handful of the mix and, over the sink, squeeze the almighty hell out of it (well, don't do yourself an injury, but it is kind of important or else the rosti won't hold together). Put your raw veg ball to one side, grab another handful and repeat until the bowl is empty. Give it a quick wipe dry and toss all the balls back in there.

○ Add the rosemary, give it a generous season and a quick shuffle-fluff with your fingertips/a fork to break the compacted balls back into strands.

○ Put a heavy-based ovenproof pan, about 20–25cm wide, on a high heat, then when it's properly hot, reduce the heat to medium for a couple of minutes to take the edge off.

○ Melt 1 tablespoon of the animal fat in the pan and once it's hot, pile in the grated mix and use a palette knife to gently but firmly press it down evenly all over.

○ As the rosti is picking up some good colour on its underside, take the time to tidy up the edges using the rounded tip to tap in the stray strands around the edge to make it into a perfect circle with no straggly bits (this last step isn't just me being anal – any bits sticking out of the main body of the rosti will burn in the oven).

○ Once your sides are tucked in and tidy, dot the other tablespoon of fat in five or so little pieces around the outside of the pan.

○ As you're watching them fizzle and slip under the rosti, keep a close eye on the very edge of it: when you see the outside couple of millimetres starting to brown, lay a lightly oiled plate on top of the pan, flip it over, then slide the rosti back in there and put back on the heat. Sounds terrifying, but is actually quite simple (as long as you're not weak-wristed).

○ Keep on the hob for another 3ish minutes to crisp up the bottom, then fling in the oven (top shelf) for 10–12 minutes to cook through.

○ Test it's ready by sticking a small knife into the centre and checking it's tender, then turn out and serve immediately.

Timeline

2 HOURS BEFORE:
You want to eat the pork once it's out and rested, and it takes no more than 10 mins to get in the oven

30 MINS BEFORE THE PIG IS COOKED:
Launch yourself into your rosti

NEXT DAY:
Different kind of pie time!

A DIFFERENT KIND OF PORK PIE

FOR THE FILLING

some cooked pork – anywhere
    north of 200g

any veg and prunes you've got left
    over from the roasting tray

1 heaped tablespoon butter

1 tablespoon plain flour

250ml chicken stock

a small handful of flat-leaf parsley,
    chopped

1 tablespoon red wine vinegar

1/2 teaspoon ground coriander

pinch of ground allspice

S & P

FOR THE CRUST

300g shortcrust pastry

plain flour, for dusting

1 egg, mixed with 1 tablespoon
    milk, for the eggwash

You will also need a shallow
    pie dish, 22cm across and
    3–4cm deep.

○ Preheat the oven to 200°C/180°C fan/gas mark 6.

○ First make the filling: take your pork out of the fridge and roughly chop along with any leftover veg and prunes.

○ Make a roux – melt the butter in a small pan over a gentle heat and briskly mix in the flour to form a rough paste. Add a good splash of the stock and beat to loosen, then repeat, a splash at a time, until the stock is all incorporated.

○ Now chuck in everything else in that section, season to taste and leave aside whilst you...

○ Roll out the pastry on a lightly floured surface and turn your pie dish upside down to cut the lid shape. Set to one side, then squish the remaining pastry into a ball and roll out again to line the pie dish.

○ Trim off the edges with a knife (I usually make my offcuts into a snout, but any porcine symbolism will do) fill with the porkiness, spreading it out to fill the pie tin.

○ Dip your fingers in cold water and run around the rim to wet the pastry, then pop the lid on and press the edges together with a fork to seal.

○ Eggwash the lid generously, and now's the time to stick on your piggy mascot and eggwash that too.

○ Make a discreet hole in the middle to allow steam to escape, and then bake in the centre of the oven for 30–40 minutes until golden.

sticky aromatic ribs

AROMATIC RIBS

PREP: 10 MINS • LEAVE: OVERNIGHT
• COOK: 2½ HOURS

STICKY RIB DRESSING

COOK: 10 MINS

SEASONED RICE

COOK: 15 MINS

You may be seeing a pattern emerging in this chapter: this is the third and final piggy recipe that had its debut in my erstwhile pork-centric restaurant, Blackfoot (Dec 2013–Jan 2016). From day one it was always in the top three bestsellers, and unlike most of the other dishes on the menu, this one actually made us a bit of money, that is to say, ribs are cheap compared to the premium cuts, even from a lovely Dingley Dell pig.

The ribs themselves are straightforward and gnawy, but it's the finishing sticky rib dressing topped off with a flourish of freshness – shards of spring onions and chilli – that continually earned the dish as a whole its place on the leaderboard.

And, just to save anyone with too much time on their hands writing in, yes, it's true that at Blackfoot we used to have a third scatterer along with the chilli and spring onions: slices of deep-fried garlic, crunchy and golden. I made a call to leave them out of this recipe as it was long enough already and arguably they're a bit of a cheffy touch rather than a home cook, but in truth they are good, or rather great.

I just figured it might be a step too far and I really, really want you to make these sticky ribs, but if you're that kind of extra miler, then you'll probably know how to deep-fry garlic anyway.

Great party food, and a fun family supper too with the rice and maybe even the Pecan Coleslaw on page 98 for a touch of cooling crunch.

AROMATIC RIBS

2kg pork ribs, separated,
    not in a rack

salt, to season

FOR THE PASTE

70g fresh ginger, washed, unpeeled,
    tough bits trimmed off and very
    roughly chopped

50g lemongrass, topped, tailed,
    tough outer leaves removed and
    cut into 2cm pieces

8 lime leaves

4 red chillies, seeds left in

5 cloves of garlic (20g), peeled but
    left whole

3 tablespoons fish sauce

2 tablespoons oil (first choice
    peanut, but rapeseed or
    vegetable are fine too)

3 tablespoons rice wine vinegar

2 tablespoons soy sauce
    (any apart from a very
    thick dark one)

AND THEN...

1 litre plain oil (like vegetable
    or sunflower)

3–4 spring onions, sliced
    diagonally

1–2 red chillies, seeds left in and
    sliced diagonally

○ For the paste, put the ginger, lemongrass, lime leaves, chillies and garlic in a blender and blitz as you slowly pour in the liquids.

○ Keep going for a while: the endgame is a smooth, if slightly hairy, paste and you may have to stop once or twice to push down the splattered sides in order to get it all combined.

○ Put the ribs in a clean plastic bag of some sort (watch for holes) and really get involved with your hands to make sure that all of them are well coated in the paste. Leave to marinate in the fridge overnight.

○ Next day, preheat the oven to 140°C/120°C fan/gas mark 1. Lay the ribs out in a large roasting tray in a way that they are not too piled up. Season lightly with salt and pour 400–500ml water down the side of the tray (not directly over the ribs) so that the bottom of the tray is just covered to a depth of 1cm but no more.

○ Double-foil the tray tightly and cook in the oven for about 2 hours, or until the meat is very tender and just beginning to come away from the bone.

○ Use tongs to gently lift the ribs out and set aside to cool, then once they are at room temp, put them in the fridge – they fry better fridge-cold.

○ Meanwhile, pour the liquor in the bottom of the tray into a wide-ish saucepan, and now swing your eyes right to the Sticky Rib Dressing...

○ When you're 15 minutes or so from serving, pour the oil into a large, high-sided saucepan – ideally it will come about halfway up. Put on a high heat and get the oil hot enough so that when you gently lower in your test rib, it floats and bubbles – roughly 180°C.

○ Working in two to three batches, depending on the size of your pan, fry the ribs until golden brown and crispy – about 5–8 minutes – then lift out with tongs or a slotted spoon and rest on a baking tray lined with kitchen paper. Once all the ribs are cooked and degreased, move them over to your serving dish/a board.

○ Spoon the sticky rib dressing over and around, and finish with the elegant obliques of spring onions and chillies.

STICKY RIB DRESSING

the rib cooking liquor

75g caster sugar

juice of 1–2 limes

1½ tablespoons dark soy sauce

○ First off, try to degrease the cooking liquor a bit by either carefully skimming or using kitchen roll to soak up the fat off the top: no need to be too obsessional, but depending on the ribs a lot of fat might have come out of them and, although it's good flavour, you really just don't need all of it.

○ Bring to a steady bubble, then stir in the sugar and leave to reduce… what you're looking for is a sticky but pourable syrup – it's a tough one to call as the consistency will change so much as it cools down: you don't want it too thin that it won't adhere to the ribs nor too reduced that it'll turn to toffee as it cools.

○ My best guidelines are that it should hit the perfect flavour/viscosity mark once it's reduced to around 100ml – about a ramekinful – and should take about 10 minutes to do so.

○ Turn the heat off, stir in the lime juice and soy sauce, then taste for a bit more of either before you spoon it over the ribs.

SEASONED RICE (See Yellow Duck Curry on page 39)

Timeline

A DAY (OR TWO) BEFORE RIB-EATING DAY

Make the paste and marinate the ribs

ON RIB DAY (OR THE DAY BEFORE IF YOU'RE REALLY AHEAD OF THE GAME)

Braise the ribs in the oven; once cooked, drain off the cooking liquor, cool to room temp, then put in the fridge to chill, along with the cooking liquor if you're working a day ahead

HALF AN HOUR BEFORE CHOW-DOWN

Get the rice on

Put the rib-frying oil on

Reduce sticky rib sauce

Fry ribs and finish rice with dressing

Slice spring onions and chilli for the final flourish

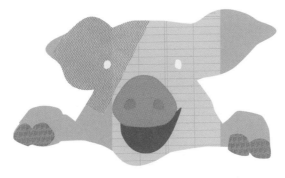

PORK **113**

chapter five

fish

As I laid out at the beginning of the book, the slow aspect in the title doesn't always refer to slow cooking, more about a passing of time, and never was that truer than in this and the seafood chapter that follows. By virtue of their very being, the goodies from the seas are quick to cook, so I've built my Slows around their marinades and accompaniments.

What occurs in the upcoming pages is a good exercise on different ways to serve up this freshest of foods – something for everyone and for most occasions, hopefully. Our menu covers big whole fish, little whole fish, raw fish, whole fillets and portioned fillets, which kind of covers it in my book... which this is. There's a distinctly Med feel to the chapter, but with a couple of stretches East and West for a mind-bogglingly simple Asian salmon dish and an utterly zippy South American ceviche.

And as well as the stars of the shows, there as some pretty unmissable sauces and sides. A take on the Potato Lovelies on page 122 is now a weekly fixture at our supper table, and the Aji Verde (see page 135) is simply one of my favourite discoveries of the year. But first up are the Agrodolce Slow-baked Tomatoes that here are served up against grilled sardines, but are just as much at home snuggled up to chicken or lamb, or in a salad, or just as they are for an antipasto on a bit of toast. Sorry, bruschetta. Not only sweet and sour but supple in their versatility too.

sardines on sourdough with agrodolce tomatoes

AGRODOLCE SLOW-BAKED TOMATOES

PREP: 10 MINS · COOK: 2½ HOURS

SARDINES ON SOURDOUGH BRUSCHETTA

PREP: 5 MINS · COOK: 15 MINS

FENNEL & OLIVE SALAD

PREP: 10 MINS

In the chit-chat of life when I say to folks I'm a chef, the next question inevitably, and perfectly reasonably, is 'Oh great! What kind of food do you do?' Well, for many pro cooks that's actually quite a hard one, because these days it's often less about chefs specialising in one cuisine, like in the good ole days before airplanes. Instead, lots of us do 'a bit of this and a bit of that' from all over the world (though not necessarily in a fusion way).

But as an answer that is just Deeply Unsatisfying For All Parties, I tend to say, with smiley false confidence, 'I do Bold Flavours', hoping that's enough to deter them from asking anything else, and following it up quickly with 'And what do you do?'.

Because really, or rather mostly, that is what I do. All of which really is just a rather verbose, wiggly way of introducing this recipe...

This is a dish of simple flavours, not especially bold, just as they should be. In fact, I hardly think this qualifies as my recipe at all; all I've done is steer three components into the same kitchen that belong together anyway.

It comes to you from way down Southern Italy. Agrodolce is their way of doing sweet and sour – a literal translation too – and it's these intense, heat-concentrated, slow-baked tomatoes that are the deep red heart of this simple yet special Mediterranean meal.

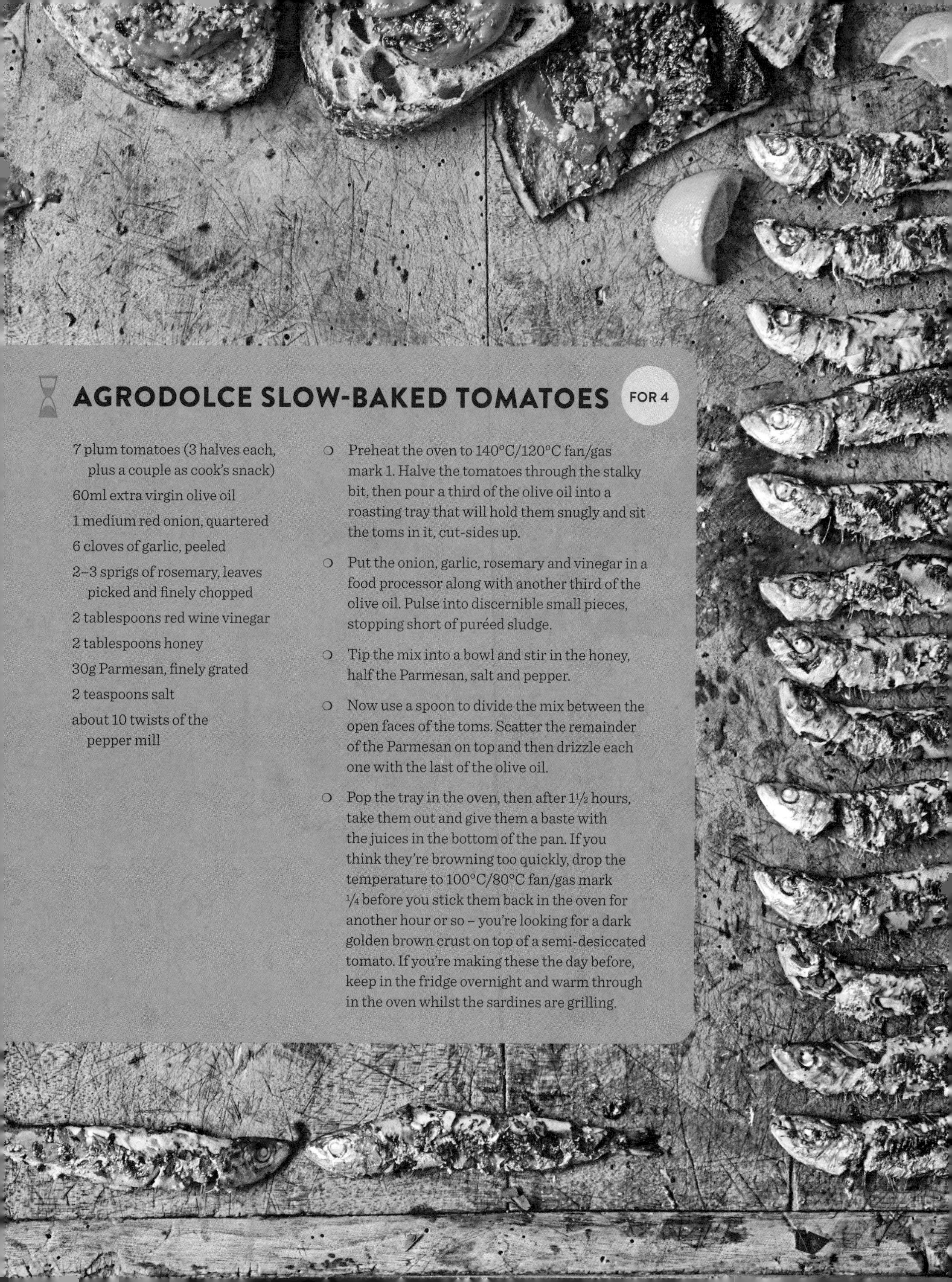

AGRODOLCE SLOW-BAKED TOMATOES

FOR 4

7 plum tomatoes (3 halves each, plus a couple as cook's snack)

60ml extra virgin olive oil

1 medium red onion, quartered

6 cloves of garlic, peeled

2–3 sprigs of rosemary, leaves picked and finely chopped

2 tablespoons red wine vinegar

2 tablespoons honey

30g Parmesan, finely grated

2 teaspoons salt

about 10 twists of the pepper mill

○ Preheat the oven to 140°C/120°C fan/gas mark 1. Halve the tomatoes through the stalky bit, then pour a third of the olive oil into a roasting tray that will hold them snugly and sit the toms in it, cut-sides up.

○ Put the onion, garlic, rosemary and vinegar in a food processor along with another third of the olive oil. Pulse into discernible small pieces, stopping short of puréed sludge.

○ Tip the mix into a bowl and stir in the honey, half the Parmesan, salt and pepper.

○ Now use a spoon to divide the mix between the open faces of the toms. Scatter the remainder of the Parmesan on top and then drizzle each one with the last of the olive oil.

○ Pop the tray in the oven, then after 1½ hours, take them out and give them a baste with the juices in the bottom of the pan. If you think they're browning too quickly, drop the temperature to 100°C/80°C fan/gas mark ¼ before you stick them back in the oven for another hour or so – you're looking for a dark golden brown crust on top of a semi-desiccated tomato. If you're making these the day before, keep in the fridge overnight and warm through in the oven whilst the sardines are grilling.

SARDINES ON SOURDOUGH BRUSCHETTA

the right amount of sardines for 2 (mains) or 4 (starters) – sardines vary wildly in size, depending on where they're from/time of year, so just tell your fishmonger how many people you're cooking for; and whilst you're there, get him to gut them, too

several sloshes of extra virgin olive oil (probably about 40ml in total)

4 thickish slices good sourdough

1 clove of garlic, peeled

S & P

TO SERVE

Agrodolce Slow-baked Tomatoes (see previous page)

2 lemons, quartered

a fat handful of flat-leaf parsley, very roughly chopped

NB: For the true taste of the Med, you'll really want to do this on a griddle/BBQ, i.e. grill lines, bit of char and that enticing fresh-fish-on-the-grill smokiness in the air...

○ Preheat the oven to 160°C/140°C fan/gas mark 3 and put a griddle/skillet on a high heat (across two if it's a bloody big one like mine). If your toms need warming up, then stick them in the oven now, along with your chosen serving dish (I like to do this as one dish in the middle of the table for looks and ease of operation).

○ Whilst the world is coming up to temp, lay out the sardines, season well on both sides and in the gut cavity, and drizzle very lightly with olive oil. Use your hands or a pastry brush to give them just the lightest of coats to stop them from sticking on the griddle – too much and you'll smoke yourselves out and taint the flavour of their flesh.

○ By now the griddle should be smoking hot, so lay down the bread on the griddle – doesn't matter if you have to do it in two loads. Grill until both sides are nicely marked, then take off and immediately use the clove of garlic to make an 'X' across each one, then put in the oven.

○ Repeat with the other slices of bread if necessary, and before you get going with those badboy sardines, lay your mitts on your best flippy thing (mine's called 'Special Flipper') – you want it to be nice and thin, so head more for a palette knife than one of those crap thick plastic shovel-things that laughably are sold as fish slices.

○ Lay as many sardines as you can on the grill – you only need to leave about 1cm between them so you can get underneath them to flip.

○ Cook for 2–3 minutes on full whack. Meanwhile, get everything out of the oven and start to pull it together: put the bruschetta out on a work surface and give them a hefty drizzle of your best extra virgin as well as a bit of a season (sea salt and freshly cracked black pepper a must for this one).

○ Round about now the sardines will be ready to be turned and the key thing is that they will tell you when they're up for it – the skin will come away from the grill with just a little encouragement, but if they're not ready yet then it will tear, in which case just lay it down again and try again in another minute. The trick is to go in gingerly and delicately and see if she's good to go, then if you get the green light, move like a dervish to flip them all as quickly as possible. Cook for the same amount of time again (the second side is always easier, as by now the griddle is well oiled).

○ As the sardines are heading for the finishing line, turn your attention back to the bruschetta: roughly smush a tomato or two on each bruschetta, then pile the whole lot up on the warmed serving dish.

○ Finish your plate of fabulousness with sardines, lemons, more olive oil (of course) and a happy scattering of parsley.

FENNEL & OLIVE SALAD

1 big or 2 small (350g) fennel bulbs

40g watercress

80g decent black olives (better to buy them with stones as they have a much better flavour, then stone them)

a small handful of sunflower seeds

20g flat-leaf parsley, leaves picked and washed

juice of ½–1 lemon

good glug (2–3 tablespoons) of extra virgin olive oil

S & P

○ Cut each fennel bulb in half, remove the core with two diagonal cuts, then slice into thin shards.

○ Toss the fennel and watercress together in a mixing bowl with the olives, seeds, parsley, lemon juice (just use half to start), olive oil and seasoning.

○ Taste and sharpen to your liking.

Timeline

A FEW HOURS EARLIER ON THE DAY (THOUGH NOTHING WRONG WITH THE DAY BEFORE)

Make toms to fruition

ABOUT AN HOUR BEFORE THE BELL

Knock up the salad but don't dress (and warm through toms if necessary)

20 MINUTES BEFORE THE BELL

Start grilling the bread, closely followed by the sardines

ONCE SARDINES ARE READY

Dress salad...and either you can squish the toms on the toast or let folks do it for themselves (I'd opt for the latter, after you've given them a demo)

fisherman's
friend

fisherman's friend

POTATO LOVELIES

PREP: 10 MINS · COOK: 3½ HOURS

BRILL GRILLED GRILLED BRILL BRILL GRILLED GRILLED BRILL

COOK: 3 MINS

ANCHOVY AIOLI

PREP: 10 MINS

It's not surprising that brill is known in the industry as the Fisherman's Favourite. Its flesh is a beautiful translucent grey with a touch of duck-egg blue, moving as it cooks into the purest white you'll ever see. The feel and taste are both masculinely meaty and femininely gentle. Something for everyone.

And as for the Lovelies... my good chef friend Mairead O'Neill gave this much-loved basic concept the perfect name, and boy did she nail it. What's not to like about a twice-baked spud loaded with butter, cream and cheese that's chewy on the outside and fluffy-rich inside? She's been serving them up for years to the trainee nurses she cooks for as well as her lovely daughter Ella, tweaking the recipe according to her audience. When I read it on her menu the idea was simply too lovely for me not to nick, and all I've done is chuck in a handful of capers and the Anchovy Aioli on the side to make supper splendiferously brill!

(NB1: Of course to turn this slow into a quick you can microwave the spuds, but as you know the skin just isn't the same.)

(NB2: I usually chuck a third spud in there too and up the rest of the ingredients a bit for a passing snack the next day, or a down payment on whatever tomorrow's sups is... these lovelies are super-versatile.)

POTATO LOVELIES

FOR 4 FOR LUNCH, 2 FOR SUPS

2 baking potatoes

100g shallots (4ish), finely chopped

2 tablespoons capers, roughly chopped

a handful of flat-leaf parsley, roughly chopped

25g butter

2 tablespoons double cream or crème fraîche

small nugget (20g) of Parmesan, finely grated

S & P

○ Preheat the oven to 180°C/160°C fan/gas mark 4. Wash the spuds, sprinkle some salt on the outside, then put directly on the oven shelf and cook for 2ish hours, dropping the temperature to 160°C/140°C fan/gas mark 3 after an hour until they are squidgy when you squeeze them (use an oven cloth, you banana).

○ Take the spuds out, leaving the oven on, and set them aside to cool for a bit, though whilst they're still warm, cut them in half and scoop their innards into a bowl.

○ Mix with all the other ingredients, except the cheese, beating the mix well to properly fluff it up, then loosely pack it back into the skins and scatter with the Parmesan.

○ Pop back in the oven and bake for 30 minutes until golden brown on top and lovely all over.

BRILL GRILLED
GRILLED BRILL
BRILL GRILLED
GRILLED BRILL

LIGHTER LUNCH FOR 4 OR PROPER SUPPER FOR 2, AND EITHER WAY I'D BACK IT UP WITH A GREEN SALAD

Timeline

2-3 HOURS BEFORE
Spuds in to bake

ANYTIME FROM NOW TO JUST BEFORE THE BRILL GOES UNDER THE GRILL
Knock up the aioli

ONCE YOU'VE TURNED THE SPUDS INTO LOVELIES AND PUT THEM BACK IN THE OVEN
Preheat the grill (last chance saloon to make the aioli)

5 MINS BEFORE
Grill Brill and off you go

4 x 120–150g brill fillets, skinned (size depends on your appetite as well as what Neptune has offered up that day)

1 tablespoon butter, softened

S (no P)

○ Preheat the grill to bloody hot and line the tray with foil.

○ Lay the brill fillets directly on the rack and use the back of a teaspoon to spread with the butter.

○ Season with just salt for the pure look, and put under the super-hot grill for 3 minutes until the flesh has gone white and they are firm yet soft to touch (like me). At this point they are Done – no need to turn over – just get them out of there onto warmed plates.

ANCHOVY AIOLI

MAKES ENOUGH FOR BRILL SUPPER, PLUS SNACKING FOR A FEW DAYS AFTER – GREAT WITH VEG STICKS, AKA CRUDITÉS

2 egg yolks

3 good-sized cloves of garlic, roughly chopped

35g anchovy fillets, plus 2 tablespoons of the oil they're in

2 tablespoons lemon juice

1 teaspoon wholegrain mustard

250ml olive oil (ideally half extra virgin and half regular)

freshly ground black pepper

○ Mayo theory for this one: put the yolks, garlic, anchos (without their oil), lemon juice and mustard in a food processor and whizz for a minute or two to bring it all together and aerate.

○ With the processor still running, slowly start adding the oils (including the anchovy oil) – which you can mix together before you start pouring if you want – until all is emulsified, then season with plenty of black pepper.

herb-baked hake

herb-baked hake

SLASH & STUFFED FISH

PREP: 20 MINS · LEAVE: OVERNIGHT · COOK: 25 MINS

YOUNG POTATOES, VIRGIN OIL

COOK: 20 MINS

A GREEK IN PHALANXES/ CHOPPED GREEK

PREP: 20 MINS

This may be Book Seven for me, but it's the first time I've written a recipe with hake... and now I feel sad I've been missing out. It all started (or rather ended) with a bad bone experience at an age when I wasn't quite experienced enough to manage them properly. And then there was that scarring time at the Cordon Bleu with a hake mousseline...

When this dish was at the concept stage, I knew it called for a Whole Big Fish, and so I looked around at the usual options and rejected them for being too expensive (turbot), too flat (halibut) or too salmony (salmon).

What about hake, said Tony, my handsome fishmonger, and I thought, well, what about hake? With the first forkful less than a day later, I knew instantly that our thirty-year feud was over. Bloody delicious; not only does the flesh have its own great flavour, but also overnight it kindly takes on the flavours of the herby marinade most welcomingly.

Our Greek salad is like one of the streets on their famous islands, cobbled, or at a stretch Cobbed, that is to say in salad vernacular, chopped up small and presented in lines, or phalanxes as they called them in ancient Greek military manoeuvres (and I always say a cookbook ain't a cookbook without a mention of ancient Greek military manoeuvres).

Quite simply, don't underestimate the delightful change of eating this greatest of salads in manageable mouthfuls, as opposed to large and unruly. You won't know until you try it and then you'll get this subliminal sense of relief – what I call a shoulders-down moment.

The final player in our three-pronged attack on your taste buds involves both youth and virginity... that is to say new potatoes in plenty of great olive oil.

SLASH & STUFFED FISH

FOR 6-8

2–2.5kg hake, gutted weight, fins trimmed and tail snipped

couple of good splashes of olive oil

couple of lemons, cut into quarters, to serve

FOR THE HERB STUFFING

zest of 3 lemons

1½ tablespoons ground fennel seeds

CONTINUED OPPOSITE

○ First make the herb stuffing by just mixing everything together in a little bowl, remembering to keep the dill fronds for the potatoes.

○ Lay the fish on one side and choose a longish knife with a thin blade; do what you can to make it as sharp as possible, as hake flesh isn't the firmest and you don't want to squish it whilst making the incisions.

○ Starting about 5cm down from the head and angling the blade towards it, make eightish evenly spaced cuts down the length of the fillet, each time making sure that you cut all the way in until you hit the backbone.

○ Divide the stuffing in half and share one half between these cuts, using the tips of your fingers to really penetrate the flesh all the way through. Carefully turn the fish over and do the same on the other side.

3 good-sized cloves of garlic (15g),
   finely chopped

30g dill, stalks chopped, fronds
   put aside for the accompanying
   spuds

25g flat-leaf parsley, leaves picked
   and chopped

1½ teaspoons sea salt

good few twists of the
   pepper mill

○ The upside to not being the firmest-fleshed
   fish is that it's quite malleable, so bend it as
   much as you can, then go about finding a
   vessel that will both contain the fish and fit
   in your fridge.

○ Clingfilm it tightly and leave in the fridge
   overnight for the pungent stuffing to pervade
   and perfume the flesh of the fish.

○ The next day, preheat the oven to
   220°C/200°C fan/gas mark 7 and get out
   your Sunday lunch roasting tray. Splash a
   couple of tablespoons of olive oil into the
   bottom of it followed by the same amount of
   water, and give it a swirl so all the base is wet.

○ Move the hake in there so it's sitting up (i.e.
   in the same position it would swim in if it
   wasn't slashed, stuffed and well dead), lightly
   oil its skin and sprinkle with sea salt.

○ Bake for 20—25 minutes, putting a suitably
   resplendent serving dish in there for the last
   couple of minutes to warm through, then
   take out and check it's done by inserting a
   skewer into the thickest part of the flesh just
   behind the head. Go all the way in until you
   hit bone, leave it there for a count of five, then
   take out and gingerly touch it onto your top
   lip. There's no way it's going to burn you but
   you do want it to be actively hot rather than
   armpit warm, so whack it back in for another
   few minutes if necessary.

○ When you're happy she's up for it, grab some
   suitable tools (fish slice/wide palette knife/
   cake slice/special flipper) and maybe a
   buddy too, as even when cooked she can be
   a bit floppy.

○ Move onto the warmed dish, pile up some
   lemon quarters and thar she blows.

Timeline

A DAY BEFORE

Make herb marinade;
slash and stuff hake

**AN HOUR+ BEFORE
YOU WANT THE HAKE
ON THE TABLE**

Chop and assemble
the Greek salad but do
not dress

**HALF AN HOUR
BEFORE SERVING**

Get the spuds on and
preheat the oven to
spanking

Once the oven is up to
speed, pop the hake in

When the spuds
are cooked, drain
and finish

Only when hake and
spuds are on the table
do you dress the salad

YOUNG POTATOES, VIRGIN OIL

1.2kg new potatoes (the younger, the better)

150ml best extra virgin olive oil you can get your hands on

2 tablespoons capers, whole if small or roughly chopped if biggies

dill fronds put aside from the hake stuffing, very roughly chopped

plenty of S & P

○ Cook the newies... you know the drill: cover with cold water and a good grab of salt, lid on, bring to the boil, take the lid off, then reduce to a busy simmer till a knife goes in without resistance, about 15 minutes.

○ Drain in a colander, put the pan back on the hob to dry, then very gently warm through half the olive oil and the capers.

○ When the spuds have had a decent 3 minute steam-dry, tip them in, turn the heat off and in a controlled manner go at them with a masher. Once they have sucked up all the oily goodness, slosh in pretty much all the remaining oil, along with most of the dill and a judicial amount of seasoning. Taste, re-season, and serve up with the last of the fronds and cascading waterfalls of liquid gold ... or green, depending on where your olive oil is from.

A GREEK IN PHALANXES

1 cucumber

2 romaine hearts or 1 large cos lettuce, sliced, washed and spun

200g black or purple salty olives (like Kalamata), stoned weight, very roughly chopped

3–4 pickled green chillies (optional, but fun)

2 x 200g packs feta, crumbled

6 RIPE vine-ripened tomatoes, diced

1 green pepper, deseeded and finely diced

1 small red onion, finely chopped

20g mint, leaves picked and roughly chopped

10g flat-leaf parsley, leaves picked and roughly chopped

1 teaspoon dried oregano

S & P

FOR THE DRESSING

around 80ml extra virgin olive oil

3 tablespoons red wine vinegar

juice of ½ lemon

○ Whisk together the dressing ingredients in a little bowl, or go for the shaken jam jar method if you prefer, adding seasoning to taste.

○ Peel the cucumber, cut it in half lengthways, then use a teaspoon to scrape out the seeds and slice the flesh into crescents.

○ Find yourself a big flattish dish and spread the lettuce mix all over the bottom of it (yup, it's a 'bed of lettuce' moment).

○ Now get military on your lines: the visual is best on this if you keep it pretty tidy. It doesn't matter what order they go in really, it's just about contrasting colours and shapes, but just for sake of ease, left to right go olives, cucumber mixed with the pickled chillies (if using), feta, toms, green pepper, red onion and finally the fresh herbs mixed together.

○ Finish by sprinkling the oregano just over the feta, a little sea salt just on the toms and a couple of cracks of black pepper over the whole lot.

○ Once you're all lined up and good to go, give the dressing a re-shake/whisk and pour all over: this one needs to be dressed not tossed, obviously.

whiskey & ginger salmon

WHISKEY & GINGER SALMON

PREP: 5 MINS · LEAVE: OVERNIGHT · COOK: 30 MINS

BINKY'S WHISKEY CARROTS & BROCCOLI

PREP: 5 MINS · COOK: 5 MINS

SEASONED RICE

COOK: 15 MINS

I've just realised that unwittingly this is one of two gingery dishes in the book that are based on my favourite cocktails: alongside the Dark & Stormy Gingerbread (pages 197–201), this is what happens when a Whiskey Mac meets a side of salmon holding a handful of broccoli. And although the gingerbread is a close, if slightly inbred, cousin of that fabulous Caribbean classic, this dish is more like a remote Asian relative: apart from in its DNA it bears no resemblance at all to my all-time top Christmas tipple.

The salmon is super-easy: marinate overnight, grill ferociously for not very long and off you go; the veg can be prepped ahead of time and cooked in a flash too, so all in all it's a gift of a meal for anyone who enjoys hosting but doesn't have all the time in the world (like my big sister Binky). For exactly those reasons, I've served this winning dish up a lot, from Inter-generational Sunday lunches to Ladies' Book Clubs (not mine) to Moroccan men folk, and have yet to find anyone who's not wowed by it. It's one of those meals that looks like you've put in so much more effort than is the case... and of course we all lurve those.

And in the unlikely event that you have any fish left over, it's really rather excellent flaked into a salad the next day.

Timeline

A DAY OR TWO AHEAD OF TIME (DEPENDING ON THE FRESHNESS OF YOUR FISH)

Marinate salmon

HALF AN HOUR BEFORE SERVING

Reduce marinade

Prep veg and get the rice on

10 MINS BEFORE SERVING

Preheat grill to combustingly hot, and get veg going on the stovetop

Once the grill is up to speed, whack the salmon under, then pay attention to finishing the veg and dressing the rice

WHISKEY & GINGER SALMON

1 salmon fillet (about 1kg), skin on,
scaled and pin-boned

FOR THE MARINADE

100ml whiskey (any will do but
you know the old one about
the better the ingredients...
spectacular with a Single Malt)

20g fresh ginger, trimmed but
unpeeled, then grated on the
big holes

130ml dark soy sauce

1 small red chilli, deseeded and
sliced

2 cloves of garlic, minced

1 tablespoon fish sauce

65g honey

splash of plain oil

TO FINISH

120ml mirin

6 limes, 2 zested and juiced, the
rest quartered for serving

○ Mix together all the ingredients for the marinade and pour into a
ceramic dish/roasting tray/container that will fit the salmon snugly.

○ Lay the fish in, skin-side up, so the flesh is properly involved in the
marinade. Cover with clingfilm and put in the fridge for a night OR
TWO if you know the fish is super-fresh (i.e. from a good fishmonger).

○ When you're about 30 minutes away from salmon serving time,
pour the marinade off the salmon into a saucepan and add the mirin
plus the lime zest and juice. Simmer over a medium heat until it
has reduced by two-thirds to a glaze consistency (about 80ml – an
espresso cup full to the top), which should take about 20 minutes,
depending on your choice of pan. Turn off the heat so it can cool a bit,
whack the grill on to high and foil the grill tray.

○ Once the sauce is ready, drizzle a little plain oil onto the foil and flip
the salmon over onto it so it's skin-side down. Grill hard and fast
for 5–10 minutes (depending on the ferocity of your grill) until it's
attractively blackened but still a bit soft when you prod it (i.e. pinkish
in the middle). NB: Grills are wildly variable, and if you find it's
blackening too much before it's cooked to your liking in the middle, use
fish slices/palette knives/slotted spoons/a lot of nerve/a mate to flip it
over and cook for a few minutes skin-side up.

○ When you're happy with the cooking and the colour, move it onto
whatever you're going to serve it on using the aforementioned
armoury, then spoon most of the reduced sauce over the top, saving
some to hit each portion with along with halved limes.

BINKY'S WHISKEY CARROTS & BROCCOLI

60g butter

300g tenderstem broccoli, stalks
trimmed and thick ones split

about 4 decent-sized carrots
(400g), peeled then shaved into
ribbons with a peeler

100ml whiskey (... plus more to
taste!)

1 teaspoon honey

S & P

○ Melt the butter in a large pan, add the broccoli and carrots and season
with salt and black pepper.

○ Roughly turn for just a couple of minutes, get the heat up, then add the
whiskey.

○ When it is sizzling, put the lid on for a minute to bring up to the boil,
then take the lid off and cook for another minute or two until all the
excess liquid has evaporated away.

○ Stir in the honey, taste for seasoning and we're done!

SEASONED RICE (See Yellow Duck Curry on page 39)

peruvian fish feast

peruvian fish feast

PERUVIAN CEVICHE

PREP: 10 MINS • LEAVE: OVERNIGHT

AJI VERDE

PREP: 3 MINS

AVOCADO TOSTADAS

PREP: 5 MINS • COOK: 5 MINS

In the world of Quick Quick Slow that I've been living in, a ceviche is the only dish that could qualify as both a Slow and a Quick. Some people swear by only bringing together fish and citrus in which it 'cooks' right at the last minute, but after plenty of extended research I found that I actually preferred the texture and deeper flavour of the overnight marinade. In the right temperature with the right ingredients, ceviche is just one of my favourite dishes ever.

The aji verde is simply a joy to make and eat: a light, zappy, dairy-free creamy corry sauce... done in seconds. These quantities make more than you need for this scenario, but it stays fresh for a good few days and is just a handy bugger to have in the fridge. Fine snacking with crudités or tortilla chips, or spoon it over fish or chicken to liven them up no end.

And the third aspect of this crowd-pleasing, time-friendly and un-fuck-up-able scenario is the avocado tostadas: take the base recipe and finish it to your liking. Away from the ceviche they make a fine lunch on their own topped with some chicken/refried beans/fish... but I'd always take the 3 minutes to blitz up the aji verde to go with them, because just like a party popper it never fails to deliver.

 ## PERUVIAN CEVICHE

FOR 4

400g spanking-fresh fish, filleted, skinned and boned (see note)

4 fat fresh King prawns, raw, peeled, deveined and halved lengthways

FOR THE CURE

120ml lime juice

50ml lemon juice

1 small clove of garlic, finely chopped

30g fresh coriander, chopped

1 fat stick of celery, finely diced

2 chillies (ideally 1 green and 1 red), deseeded and sliced (quite fiery... use less if you prefer!)

S & P

In Peru, they'd most likely use corvina, or sea bass as we call it, for this, but any firm-fleshed white fish works fine, i.e. bream. I've also done it with yellowtail hamachi tuna – expensive but fabulous.

○ Trim any excess fatty bits from around the edge of the fillet(s), then dice the flesh into 1–2cm squares (or ask your fishmonger to do it).

○ Put into a bowl with the prawns and all the cure ingredients, give it a good stir, cover tightly with clingfilm and leave to sit in the fridge overnight.

○ Just before serving, drain, saving the juice for a lucky cook's treat – it's great in a shot with a splash of Pisco!

○ Season the fish with salt and pepper, then taste – more salt or lime juice may be required... and this dish needs to be seriously on point.

○ Serve with the aji verde, tostadas and some tortilla chips on the side.

AJI VERDE

100g coriander (including stalks), washed, patted dry/spun and very roughly chopped

1–2 green chillies (depending on how hot you like it), deseeded and roughly chopped

2 cloves of garlic, chopped

100ml olive oil

juice of 1 lime

½–1 teaspoon salt, depending on how much of a salt fiend you are

- Put all the ingredients in a blender and whizz together until smooth.
- Taste and adjust for seasoning and overall yum factor.
- This will keep well for up to 3 days in the fridge.

AVOCADO TOSTADAS

FOR 4

2 ripe avocados, halved, stoned and scraped out

zest and juice of 1 lime

4 x 20cm tortillas (corn or flour ones... your call)

150g cherry tomatoes (15ish), halved or quartered, depending on size and time

60g ricotta or soured cream

a handful of coriander, chopped

S & P

- Preheat the grill to good and hot. In a bowl, roughly smash the avocado flesh with a fork, then stir in the lime zest and juice and seasoning to taste.
- Grill the tortillas for a couple of minutes until they are hot and hard – you need to be able to pick them up without them flopping.
- Gently spread the smashed avo on top so as not to break the tortillas, share the cherry tomatoes between them, dollop the ricotta on in blobettes and round it all off with the chopped corry.

Timeline

NIGHT BEFORE
Marinate ceviche

AS YOU APPROACH EL MOMENTO DE CEVICHE

First take a few mins for aji verde, then turn your attention to the tostadas (also a good moment to delegate the Pisco sour-making duties)

Last *trabajo* is to drain and season the fish

chapter six
seafood

Crab, mussels, prawns, scallops and squid. A fine landing of seafood by anyone's standards, but it's only fair to comment that none of it particularly enjoys anything more than the fastest of times in the hotspot. Unless you're one of those folks who sous-vides at a precisely probed-roundabout-armpit-temperature (and if you are I'm not sure what you're doing here) in the great Venn diagram of cookery, the intersection between slow cooking and seafood is a small, bordering on non-existent one.

So in this chapter we find ourselves mostly reliant on third parties for our slows: the squid is made excellent with an infused oil that delivers a truly eye-opening mayo. The soft, sweetness of scallops is contrasted with crunchy veg, lightly pickled overnight. Our prawns excel against a backdrop permeated by home-made preserved lemons, and a Belgian classic of mussels and beer is doubled up with a loaf of crusty beer-based bread.

Thus it's our crab alone that delivers the slow-cooked premise and promise on the front cover, and even then it's not the heat-sensitive meat that goes the long haul, but its flavoursome exoskeleton which forms the backbone of the Number One dish in this book – flip to page 148 to see why it gets the top spot...

Squid with Szechuan mayo & blackened tenderstem

SZECHUAN-CHILLI MAYO

COOK: 25 MINS • LEAVE: 1 WEEK (OR 1 MONTH!) • PREP: 5 MINS

BLACKENED TENDERSTEM WITH SESAME & GARLIC

PREP: 5 MINS • COOK: 10 MINS

CRUNCH 'N' CHEW SQUID

PREP: 10 MINS • COOK: 5 MINS

Hold the front page! In the world of 'condiments that go viral', the Szechuan chilli mayo that supports the crunchy squid in these recipes may just be the next red onion marmalade or chipotle ketchup. Who knew it was going to turn out to be such a winner? Yes, yes, you have to set it up about a week (or a month) in advance, but for something that takes so little effort to throw together, the result is exceedingly gratifying. It does go particularly well with both the squid and blackened broccoli it's paired with here, but beyond that lies a world of opportunity. I just keep thinking about a soft-shell crab bun, or grilled prawns, or anything really from the sea. Or a pig.

I never understand why folks don't cook more squid at home. It tastes like holiday, is the quickest of cooks – literally just a couple of minutes on the grill or in hot oil – and cheaper than fish too. The only thing I can think is that most people don't go to a fishmonger, and you do want your squid to be fresh and whole at point of purchase, but after that you can get your fishmonger to prep it for you. It freezes really well too, so when you do next find yourself in a place of fresh fishiness, buy a few suppers worth, pack 'em up into portions and have them there when you need a quick emergency meal.

Ingredient alert: Szechuan peppercorns haven't quite hit the mainstream yet, so whilst you can get them in some (posh) supermarkets/grocers, you might have to factor in a trip to the Asian store or order them online. Sooo worth it though.

SZECHUAN-CHILLI MAYO

FOR THE INFUSED OIL

This makes enough for 5 lots of the astounding mayo and lasts for months in a cool place (not the fridge)

4 tablespoons Szechuan peppercorns

500ml peanut oil

1 bulb of garlic, unpeeled and cut in half horizontally

4 dried bird's eye chillies or ⅛ to ¼ teaspoon chilli flakes, depending on your limits

FOR THE MAYO

2 egg yolks

1 clove of garlic, minced

juice of 1 lime

100ml vegetable oil

100ml infused Szechuan oil (above), sieved to remove the aromatics

salt, to taste

○ Toast the Szechuan peppercorns in a medium-sized dry saucepan on a low heat for 3–4 minutes.

○ Add everything else to the pan and then keeping the heat low, let it bubble away slowly for 20 minutes.

○ Chuck out the garlic, but tip everything else into a jar, seal and leave for at least a week (even better a month) to infuse.

To make into a jam jarful of the yummiest mayo EVER (which also keeps in the fridge for a week)...

○ Put the yolks, garlic and lime juice in a food processor and whizz together for a minute until canary yellow. (NB: If you're using a standard-sized food processor, the volume may be a bit small to get the required good whipping, so try tipping it up towards you on two feet so the yolks, etc make a pool, which the blade can whizz through.)

○ As with any mayonnaise, slowly pour in both oils in a steady stream. Season to taste with salt, and a bit more lime juice if it needs it.

BLACKENED TENDERSTEM
WITH SESAME & GARLIC

FOR 4

2 tablespoons sesame seeds (go for a mix of regular and black if you're feeling fancy, but it's really neither here nor there)

300g tenderstem broccoli

1 tablespoon toasted sesame oil

2 cloves of garlic, chopped

1–2 tablespoons light soy sauce, to taste

○ Tip the sesame seeds into a small pan and gently toast them to proper golden brown over a low heat, flipping regularly for the 5ish minutes it'll take.

○ Put a griddle pan/wide, dry frying pan/skillet over a high heat and whilst it's getting good and hot, toss the tenderstem in a bowl with garlic and sesame oil.

○ Lay down as many stems as you can but don't pile them up. Turn after 2–3 minutes when the undersides should be a bit charred, then cook for the same amount of time on the other side.

○ Move that lot into a bowl (preferably metal so it doesn't suck the heat out of them), clingfilm tightly and get the next lot on.

○ When all is said and done, shake in the soy and toss with the sesame seeds (don't add any salt). This lot looks best piled up on something tight-fitting and flat, rather than at the bottom of a deep bowl.

CRUNCH 'N' CHEW SQUID

STARTER FOR 4, MAINS FOR 2

400g squid (combo of tubes and tentacles), cleaned weight, tubes sliced into 2–3cm rings (thinner if they're really big tubes) and tentacles cut into pieces of 2–3 dangly bits still held together at the top

1 litre vegetable oil, for frying

1 egg

80ml milk

250g semolina/fine cornmeal/fine polenta

salt, to taste

lime wedges, to serve

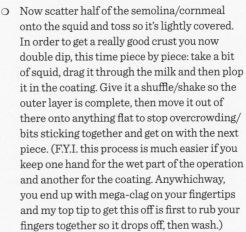

❍ Choose yourself three medium-sized mixing bowls (or something similar): whisk the egg with the milk in one, weigh the semolina/cornmeal into the another with a good pinch of salt and put the squid into the last. Pour the eggy milk onto the squid and leave to sit and soak for a minute, then tip the excess liquid back into the bowl it came from, leaving as little as possible pooling with the squid.

❍ Now scatter half of the semolina/cornmeal onto the squid and toss so it's lightly covered. In order to get a really good crust you now double dip, this time piece by piece: take a bit of squid, drag it through the milk and then plop it in the coating. Give it a shuffle/shake so the outer layer is complete, then move it out of there onto anything flat to stop overcrowding/bits sticking together and get on with the next piece. (F.Y.I. this process is much easier if you keep one hand for the wet part of the operation and another for the coating. Anywhichway, you end up with mega-clag on your fingertips and my top tip to get this off is first to rub your fingers together so it drops off, then wash.)

❍ Pour the oil into a saucepan about 20cm wide and 10cm deep, so that the oil comes roughly halfway up the side to allow room for bubbling and pop it on a high heat to get it up to temp.

❍ Prepare a tray with kitchen paper as a landing mat for the freshly fried squid.

❍ Test the oil is up to temp by dropping in a little hunk of bread, which should go into a very busy fizzle, then quick as you can, one by one, lower half the squid pieces into the hot oil and immediately give them a stir so they don't stick.

❍ Fry until golden brown, about 5 minutes, then use a slotted spoon to lift onto the kitchen paper for a quick degrease and a hefty season: it's important you hit them with a decent amount of salt before the oil on the coating stops glistening or else it won't stick properly, and as we all know, a respectful amount of salt is the yin to the yang of the deep-fat fryer.

❍ Keep the first lot warm whilst you get on with frying the rest, then tuck in sharpish.

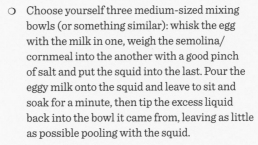

Timeline

ANYTIME FROM A DAY TO A MONTH FROM WHEN YOU NEED IT

Make the infused oil

ON THE DAY

Miraculously turn the infused oil into mayo

20 MINS-ISH BEFORE D-DAY

Toast the sesame seeds

Prep broccoli and toss with garlic and oil

Preheat griddle

Prep the squid

10 MINS BEFORE

Extraction on/windows open

Put oil on to heat for squid

Start griddling broccoli

5 MINS BEFORE

Drain then coat the squid >> fry batch 1

Finish griddling broccoli >> toss as second lot of squid working (or something like that)

mussels, beer & chips

BEER BREAD

PREP: 15 MINS • LEAVE: 2½ HOURS • COOK: 1 HOUR

MUSSELS WITH BEER & BACON

PREP: 10 MINS • COOK: 10–15 MINS

VITE FRITES

PREP: 15 MINS • COOK: 10 MINS

Mussels, chips, and some crusty, dense bread to sop up all the juice. Cracking, simple idea, and a perfect Quick Quick Slow trio. The clever bit, in terms of the recipes, was that there's a three-way tie-in from the beer the mussels are cooked in (a Belgian classic), to the beer in the bread (it's a yeast thing), to the one that you might enjoy a glass of with your fine meal.

Only problem was that when we tested both the mussels and the bread with various beers (I know, hard job), it turned out that the mussels really suited a white or wheat beer best, like Hoegaarden, whereas the lightness of that was lost in the bread, which preferred the deep, bitter flavour of a brown beer, like Leffe Brune. And that's without even going into what you'd like to imbibe on the side...

What to do? Well, if you're going to do the thing properly, then I'm going to have to recommend that you get two different beers, plus a third for you if you fancy it. Get a couple of extra bottles of each and approach it more like a Belgian beer tasting, and fairly shortly any niggles you had about my annoying beery specifications will have drifted far, far away...

 BEER BREAD

MAKES A GOOD-SIZED COTTAGE LOAF – 8–10 SLICES

330ml strong brown beer*, at room temperature

500g strong white bread flour, plus extra for dusting

2 teaspoons (8g) sea salt

1 teaspoon (3.5g/½ packet) fast-action dried yeast

olive oil, for greasing

a handful or so of big ice cubes

○ Make sure the beer is at room temperature – if it's cold, run it under the hot tap for a few minutes to warm up, as the colder the beer, the longer it will take to activate the yeast.

○ Mix together all the ingredients (except the oil and ice) in a bowl using a wooden spoon, then tip out onto your work surface, including all the still dry bits of flour, and get kneading, incorporating all the loose bits of flour to stop it sticking... plus more as necessary. Give it a good workout for 10 minutes until it starts to feel smooth and elastic, and you start to feel knackered and achy.

○ Lightly grease a large mixing bowl with some olive oil so the dough doesn't stick to it, bring the dough into a ball, give it a quick, light roll around in there just to coat the surface with oil to stop it drying

If you're staying true to the country of the dish, I'd go for something like Leffe Brune or Westmalle Dubbel, but after trying it with a range of different brown beers our fave was actually Stokey Brown from the Pressure Drop Brewery in the good old East End of London; digging the craft beer scene (as ABBA used to sing).

CONTINUED ON PAGE 144

BEER BREAD (CONTINUED)

out, cover with a damp cloth and put in a warm place (airing/boiler cupboard is ideal) to prove for a couple of hours. This one does most of its rising in the oven, so don't expect it to double in size – you're looking at more like a 20% volume increase.

○ Once it's done its thing, plop the dough onto a flour-dusted surface, knock the air out of it using your knuckles, then with your hands slightly cupped, form into a ballish shape. Put onto a lightly floured baking tray, re-oil the surface of the dough, then cover with the damp cloth again and leave at room temp (not in the airing cupboard) to prove for a further 30 minutes.

○ Preheat the oven to 190°C/170°C fan/gas mark 5. Take a moment to repeat the cupping movement to give the ball a bit of height, score the loaf with a light 'X' on top and once the oven is up to speed, put the bread on the middle shelf. Immediately throw 2–3 big ice cubes straight onto the oven floor; the steam makes all the difference to the crust.

○ It'll take about 50–60 minutes to bake, and after the first 10 minutes, open the oven door (avoiding a steam facial if possible) and throw in another couple of ice cubes, then immediately close it again.

○ It's done when the loaf sounds hollow when you tap the base. Leave it to cool completely on a rack before slicing/ hunking.

 # MUSSELS WITH BEER & BACON

30g butter

130g unsmoked lardons/pancetta, cubed

2 banana shallots, finely diced

2 cloves of garlic, sliced

8–10 sprigs of thyme, leaves picked and chopped

1.5kg fresh raw mussels in their shells, cleaned

330ml bottle of wheat beer

3 tablespoons crème fraîche

a small handful (10g) of flat-leaf parsley, roughly chopped

S & P

○ Melt the butter in a wide pan big enough to hold the mussels, with a lid that fits and as it starts to bubble, chuck in the pancetta.

○ Carry on gently frying until the fat starts coming out and it's beginning to go golden brown around the edges – up to 5 minutes.

○ Add the shallots, garlic and thyme and stir for the couple of minutes it takes for the shallots to go that lovely shade of muted pink – no browning please.

○ Tip in the mussels, give them a good roll and coat in the oniony-bacony goodness, then crank up the heat to full, pour in the beer and pop the lid on.

○ Have a peek after 3ish minutes – the mussels will probably have opened but if not all, give it a good shake to move them around, stick the lid back on and come back in another minute or two, but no longer.

○ Use a slotted spoon to lift the mussels into a warmed dish/dishes (chucking away any unopened ones), then stir the crème fraîche and parsley into the sauce.

○ Season, taste and re-season, then ladle over the waiting, expectant mussels.

FOR 2

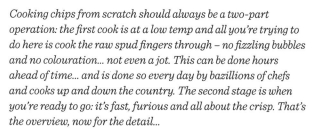

VITE FRITES

1 litre frying oil, like vegetable or cheap rapeseed oil

800g chipping potatoes, peeled and cut into chips (even if you favour fat chips, this is definitely a thinner situation, partly because chips with mussels are always on the skinnier side, and also this is supposed to be a Quick – so aim for 1 x 1cm x as long as your spud defines)

salt, to taste

Cooking chips from scratch should always be a two-part operation: the first cook is at a low temp and all you're trying to do here is cook the raw spud fingers through – no fizzling bubbles and no colouration... not even a jot. This can be done hours ahead of time... and is done so every day by bazillions of chefs and cooks up and down the country. The second stage is when you're ready to go: it's fast, furious and all about the crisp. That's the overview, now for the detail...

❍ Choose a wideish pan with high sides and pour in the oil; the oil should only come about halfway up inside (no higher as there will be a bit of bubbling later). Stick it on a low–medium heat and get on with cutting your chips.

❍ Turn your attention to the oil: if you have a kitchen thermometer you want to reduce the heat when the oil temp hits 130°C, and if you don't, then just drop a chip in and see what happens: ideally the chip will sink and with a minimal amount of bubbling slowly cook through without colouring at all. If it starts fizzling excitedly, then the oil is already too hot, so turn it down and let it cool off for a few minutes. When you're happy with the temp, carefully lower half of the chips in there, give them a stir and leave them to do their thing for about 8 minutes.

❍ Meanwhile, prepare a baking tray with a few layers of kitchen paper on it for when they come out.

❍ To check if they're ready, use a slotted spoon to lift out one solitary chip and give it a quick but firm squeeze around its middle: if it's squidgy and soft, it's ready, so carefully lift them all out and lay out in a single layer on the kitchen paper. Now repeat with the other half.

❍ Depending on where you're at on your timeline, either turn the oil off and leave it to cool until it's mussel time, or if that is now, then crank the heat up under the pan.

❍ If you have a kitchen thermometer, head for 190°C... if not, wait until your kitchen smells a little like a chip shop, then lower in a test chip: this time you want it to fizzle busily and float. Once that happens, gently lower in the half the chips and this time the oil will bubble up. Again it's important that you give the chips a shuffle around pretty immediately or else they will stick to each other and the bottom of the pan.

❍ This second fry doesn't take long at all – just a couple of minutes – so get ready with a mixing bowl lined with kitchen paper. Once the frites are golden and crispy, use a slotted spoon to move them into the bowl, then quickly repeat with the second batch. Season generously with salt, toss well to coat and then whip away the degreasing paper before they hit the table.

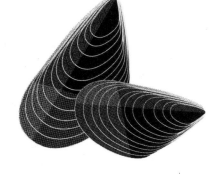

Timeline

AT LEAST 4 HOURS BEFORE
Make the dough >> prove

2 HOURS BEFORE
Knock back dough, shape and reprove at room temp

ANY TIME ABOUT NOW
Peel and cut the spuds
Blanch them, then turn off the oil
De-beard mussels and prep other ingredients

1 HOUR BEFORE
Cook bread

WHEN THE BREAD COMES OUT
Turn oil up to high for second cook of the frites ...and start frying the bacon in the mussel pan
As the beer goes into the mussels and the lid goes on, drop the chips into the bloody hot oil.
And if you're lucky/ clever they should both be done about the same time

crab laksa

PARANKAN CRAB CURRY LAKSA

PREP: 1 HOUR • COOK: 30 MINS

TAMARIND SAMBAL

PREP: 5 MINS • LEAVE: 15 MINS

CRISPY SHALLOTS

PREP: 10 MINS • COOK: 5 MINS

Parankan is the name given to folks of Chinese descent who came down and made their homes in the Straits of Malacca (Malaysia, Indonesia and Singapore). Round there, laksas come in two types: the Asam variety is defined by the sauce being sour with tamarind, and is more associated with Malaysia and Penang in particular. The other is the simply named Curry laksa, noted for its coconutty creaminess, and this recipe is based on the latter after one such bowl of marvellousness I recently had in Singapore.

This was the first dish I cooked for this book, and that was probably a good thing as it helped me refine what I wanted it to be about. To me, the idea of Slow versus Quick wasn't all about putting something in the oven and walking away, but more, as I've said before, about a passing of time: there was an action, followed by a period of inaction, before the final pull together with the accompanying quicks.

However, as I got on with making this fine laksa, I realised that it involved low-level but undeniably fairly continual action over a period of some hours. Hmmm, this is not the brief I had in mind, I thought to myself. The Quicks were and are just as I'd envisaged, but the laksa is definitely a bit of a labour of love... especially if you're the crab ,who really does give his all to it.

But I've left it in for two reasons: first and foremost, it really is worth the effort: the kind of dish that should be accompanied by sparklers as well as sambal. And secondly, it's where my Quick Quick Slow journey started, and I can't help believing that taking that first stumbling step really is as important – if not more so – than where you end up.

This pretty intense journey starts with you and a living crab and ends in a fabulous feast... and to be honest there's not a lot of respite in there. So my advice is to utilise the minutes after the crab has gone in the freezer and then whilst it's cooking to make the sambal (which does well for a bit of come-together time anyway) and attend to the seemingly indestructible Crispy Shallots.

PARANKAN CRAB CURRY LAKSA

 FOR 6

1kg male brown crab, live

4 large crab claws (about 150–200g each), raw and shells cracked with the back of a knife

○ Put the crab in the freezer for 40 minutes to go to sleep. Halfway through that time put a pan big enough to fit it in on the stove with 2.5 litres of water. Pop a lid on and bring to a rolling boil – no salt.

○ Get the crab out – he's now not quite in this world – and using your hands, break off his claws ①. Sounds mean but he won't feel it at all and in another 40 seconds he'll be dead.

○ Slip him (clawless) into the boiling water for 10 minutes, and whilst he's cooking crack the two raw claws with the back of a chunky chef's

FOR THE STOCK

250g raw, shell-on prawns
(I generally use King – fine
if they're frozen)

1 large or 2 small onions, unpeeled
and halved

1 bulb of garlic, cut in half
horizontally

2 carrots, unpeeled and halved

2 tomatoes, left whole

2 sticks of lemongrass, bashed with
the butt of a chef's knife

3cm piece of fresh ginger, cut into 3

FOR THE BASE PASTE

200g shallots, sliced

2 sticks of lemongrass, trimmed
and bottom halves sliced, tops
left whole

2 red chillies, deseeded and
roughly chopped

2 cloves of garlic, peeled and
left whole

4 lime leaves

1/2 teaspoon shrimp paste

2 tablespoons tamarind
concentrate/paste

2 tablespoons dark soy sauce

2 tablespoons fish sauce

4 tablespoons peanut oil

CONTINUED ON PAGE 150

knife ② (this is for the lucky diners to be able to access the meat later), then put with the other ones in the fridge.

○ Once cooked, lift him out with a slotted spoon. Turn the water off but don't throw it as it will be our stock base. Leave the guy to cool until handleable (doorstep/windowsill quickens the process).

○ Meanwhile, blitz the prawns for the stock in a food processor (just as they are with their heads and shells on) into a mushy paste. Tip into the crab-cooking water with the other stock ingredients and bring to a fairly busy simmer for about an hour until it has reduced down to a litre (no need to skim).

○ When the crab is cool enough to handle (10ish minutes), turn it upside down, break off the eight spindly legs ③ and put them into a bowl to add to the stock. Turn the body so that the arrow-shaped flap is closest to you, then put both of your thumbs at the very base of it and push up, ④ thus prising out the labyrinthine middle of the crab ⑤ ⑥. Therein lies the white meat: put it aside for a bit of concentrated picking laters.

○ Have a peer inside the crab shell: tip any murky water into the stock bowl, then pick out and throw away the long, soft furry bits known as devil's fingers (you'll know what I mean).

○ Tear out and chuck the transparent membrane too, then either using your fingers or a spoon, carefully scrape all the brown meat nestling inside the shell ⑥ into a bowl and put it in the fridge.

○ Once the shell is empty, chuck it and the legs in a carrier bag, bash the hell out of them with a rolling pin and tip into the simmering stock.

○ Now get on with picking the inside of your crab... gather the bits and pieces you'll need first: the bowl from before for the parts that will go into the stock, a small bowl for the crab meat, a chopping board, a chef's knife and a skewer.

○ With this lot arranged in front of you, get comfy (i.e. sit down) for the next bit. First off, cut the bone-and-meat-mass that lay in the heart of the crab in half through the middle ⑦. You'll see that basically what it consists of is lots of little chambers, each containing the yummy white meat, separated by thin bone walls. The aim of the game is to carefully use your skewer to flick and pick out all the meat without getting any bits of bone. Start methodically emptying out all the chambers ⑧ into the bowl, turning it in your hand as you go: don't be too aggressive with your poking as the shell walls are super-thin and you don't want to shatter them. Once all the chambers exposed to you are emptied, cut it again through the middle with a confident bang from your chef's knife (as opposed to sawing at it, which will splinter the shell) to expose new ones.

○ Keep going like this until you have four pretty much empty quarters of the labyrinth ⑨: weigh each one in turn in your hand and assess if you think there is more meat hidden in there, in which case cut it again and repeat.

CONTINUED ON PAGE 151

TO COMPLETE

100g sugar snaps, thinly sliced lengthways

3 spring onions, thinly sliced at an angle

½ cucumber, thinly shredded (but not the seeds)

a large handful (15g) of mint, roughly chopped

400ml tin coconut milk

100g (½ block) creamed coconut

300g flat rice noodles, or, if you're in the Asian shop, the thicker ones used specifically for laksa

juice of 1–2 limes, plus 3 for serving, halved

100g sweetcorn kernels, shucked (fresh or frozen)

3–4 regular chillies, sliced (or a couple of bird's eye if you're brave)

salt or extra soy sauce, to taste

❍ When you're looking at a satisfying pile of white crab meat and a lot of empty bone chambers, mix the white meat with the brown, and stick back in the fridge. Put the empty 'heart' pieces into the stock-destined bowl and tip it into the bubbling stock. Job done – huzzah! And now it's paste time...

❍ Pop all the ingredients for the paste in a blender and blitz till smooth, adding some water, a tablespoon at a time, to lubricate it if it gets stuck.

❍ Sit a big, wide pan over a low–medium heat, then scrape in the paste and fry gently for about 10ish minutes, stirring regularly with a spatula to stop it sticking on the bottom, until it's firmed up, i.e. not so wet.

❍ As the paste is cooking, take a few minutes to prep and mix the topper salad: sugar snaps, spring onions, cuc and mint, and put to one side.

❍ If your stock isn't down to a litre yet, then turn the paste off and hang out till it's ready. Once it's hit the mark, strain into a bowl through a sieve, giving it a really good push down to get all the flavour out.

❍ Warm the base paste up again (if necessary), pour in the reduced stock, giving it a bit of a stir to bring it together, increase the heat to high and add both kinds of coconut (milk and creamed).

❍ Once it's up to an easy simmer, sit the claws in there, put the lid on and let it all simmer gently for 8 minutes.

❍ Boil the kettle and as it comes up to speed put the noodles in a heatproof bowl. Pour on boiling water to cover and leave to sit for 5 minutes, giving them the odd poke, then drain.

❍ Season the curry to taste with lime juice and salt or extra soy.

❍ You are now ready to serve. Ideally working into shallow bowls, pile the noodles up in the middle and scatter on the raw shucked corn. Briefly mix together the brown and white meat, dollop it on followed by ladles of the hot laksa broth. Top with the shredded greens and finish with a resplendent claw.

❍ Complete the moment with the Tamarind Sambal and Crispy Shallots (see over the page), a little dish of sliced chillies and handsome halves of lime.

❍ It's the kind of special that brings a room to silence.

Timeline

FIRST THINGS FIRST
Put the crab in the freezer

WHILE HE'S IN THERE
Make the sambal
Make the crispy shallots

AFTER 40 MINS IN THE FREEZER
Cook and pick the crab

AND FINALLY
Make the curry

TAMARIND SAMBAL

80g desiccated coconut

50g tamarind concentrate

1 teaspoon dried shrimp paste,
    dissolved in 1 tablespoon
    hot water

½ teaspoon palm sugar

2 green chillies, halved, deseeded
    and finely diced

zest of 2 limes

small pinch of salt

○ Put everything into a bowl and mix well, using the back of a spoon to fully make it all become one.

○ Leave to sit to soften and come together, then taste for salt – it may not need any because of the shrimp paste (depends how salty you like it).

CRISPY SHALLOTS

about 1 litre frying oil (groundnut
    oil tastes good, but vegetable or
    sunflower is fine too)

400g shallots (about 5 banana
    shallots... sooo much less
    tedious to peel)

salt, to taste

○ Choose a high-sided pan to allow for a bit of bubbling and pour the oil into it. Prepare yourself a landing tray for after the event with a few layers of kitchen roll on it.

○ Heat the oil gently whilst you prep the shallots: once peeled, cut them into slices about 5mm thick, then tip into a mixing bowl and break them all up into individual rings. It's worth being a bit fastidious about this step as it's what will make them crisp.

○ Increase the heat under the oil to medium, and from here on in check whether it's at the right temp by chucking in a solitary ring every now and again and seeing if it fizzles effusively and floats.

○ Once you're good to go, gently tip the shallot rings in there and get stirring with a slotted spoon.

○ You don't want the oil to be too hot, so adjust the temp as necessary – it should take about 5 minutes of pretty constant stirring to get them to the colour/dehydration point you want, which is the shade after golden brown. (NB: They won't be crispy as you lift them out – they crisp up in the air over the next few minutes.)

○ Lift the rings out onto your prepared tray using a slotted spoon and immediately sprinkle with a good grab of salt.

○ Leave to cool completely, and if you're not going to use them in the next hour or so, store in an airtight container, where they'll hold steady for a good 24 hours.

DO CHUA
(VIETNAMESE PICKLES)

PREP: 15 MINS • LEAVE: OVERNIGHT

STEAMED SCALLOPS
WITH GINGER & SOY

PREP: 10 MINS • COOK: 5 MINS

TOMORROW'S BANH MI

COOK: 20 MINS • PREP: 5 MINS

steamed scallops with do chua

This trio of recipes is the most relaxed of three-day events: Day One, in a matter of minutes you whip up the shredded pickles that are the Slow at the heart of both dishes to come as they need to sit overnight.

Day Two's pride and joy is the sophisticated little scallop starter – again just minutes required in the kitchen to produce a dish of purity, simplicity and elegance.

And then with a similar amount of input, Day Three yields the kind of special sarnie that can utterly change the complexion of your afternoon.

Decent return for minimal labour, I'd wager.

 ## DO CHUA (VIETNAMESE PICKLES)

FIRST SECTION

4 regular or 3 fat carrots (300g)
(the fresher the better, i.e. not
bendy), peeled

equal weight(ish) (300g) turnips,
mouli or kohlrabi (basically
anything white and crunchy),
peeled

1½ tablespoons caster sugar

1½ teaspoons salt

SECOND SECTION

about 220ml vinegar (a 50:50 mix
of cider and rice wine vinegar is
ideal, but any will do really)

90g caster sugar

2 heaped teaspoons salt

○ Shred the veg with whatever best instrument you have: a handheld
Asian-style shredder is ideal – it looks like a speed peeler but with
vicious teeth, costs just a couple of quid and is worth every penny.
Mandolins also do the job well but are a bit more spenny, and for
you folks with a spiraliser, well, here's your chance to whip it out.
Failing all that, go for some fine knife work or as a lowest common
denominator, the big holes on the grater do a fair rendition too.

○ Once you're through that minor stress, put the shredded veg into a big
bowl with the caster sugar and salt in the first section and massage for
a couple of minutes until floppy.

○ Now rinse the veg off and give them a good squeeze in four or so
handfuls to get rid of the excess water, before putting them into a
container – ideally a jar, but Tupperware will do.

○ Give your bowl a quick rinse, then add all the ingredients in the second
section to the bowl, along with 250ml water, and stir until the sugar
has dissolved (no heat required) and there are no granular bits on
the bottom.

○ Pour it over the veg to cover, poking the veg down a bit if necessary.
Seal in whatever fashion your chosen vessel calls for and leave to
pickle-up in the fridge overnight.

STEAMED SCALLOPS WITH GINGER & SOY

12 fresh scallops, cleaned and then put back in their half shells

short thumb-sized (5cm) piece of fresh ginger, knobbly bits trimmed off, then finely grated

250ml dark soy sauce

150ml toasted sesame oil

1 x recipe Do Chua (see previous page)

spring onions, finely sliced

STARTER FOR 4, OR A MAIN IF YOU KNOCK UP SOME SEASONED RICE (SEE PAGE 39) AND BLACKENED TENDERSTEM WITH SESAME AND GARLIC (SEE PAGE 140)

○ Replicate having an army of steamer baskets by putting a cooling rack or two on the bottom of a large roasting tray and laying the scallops in their shells on it – it doesn't matter if the shells are overlapping as long as the scallops aren't covered.

○ Put a pea-sized amount of grated ginger on top of each scallop, then carefully pour 2–3cm water into the bottom of the tray, avoiding the shells. Tightly and carefully double-foil the whole thing, to make sure the steam can't escape.

○ Meanwhile, gently warm the dark soy and sesame oil in a small pan.

○ Now put the roasting tray across two burners and crank them up to full (and if you're not cooking on gas, then preheat your hob rings to full before putting the roasting tray on). After just 3 minutes, lift up a corner of the foil and have a peek – the scallops should have just gone opaque and have firmed up when you squeeze them, in which case turn the heat off, and if not, just tuck it all up tight again and put it back over the heat for just another 2 minutes.

○ Whip the foil off and drape a small handful of Do Chua about the shell – use as much as you like, but roughly speaking you should still have about a quarter (big handful) left for the Banh Mi.

○ Finish with a dessertspoonful of the soy-ses mix over each scallop and veg (you don't want or need them to be swimming in this super-powerful potion), which should leave you with about an egg cupful for tomorrow's sarnies. Last touch is a flourish of delicate spring onion shards, and away you go.

TOMORROW'S BANH MI

$\boxed{\text{FOR 2}}$

Timeline

2 part-baked demi-baguettes (you know, the ones you get from the supermarket)

50g vermicelli rice noodles

the rest of the Do Chua (see page 155)

a handful of coriander, roughly chopped

a handful of sugar snap peas/ mangetout, thinly sliced

2 spring onions, sliced

the rest of the soy-sesame sauce (from the Steamed Scallops, see opposite)

a little mayo

few leaves of baby gem (preferably outer ones)

a handful of mint leaves

a small handful of salted peanuts

juice of 1 lime

○ Preheat the oven and bake the baguettes according to the packet instructions, taking them to the far side of the cooking window (i.e. not yellow and pale, but dark golden brown and crunchy: this is a crucial part of the banh mi experience).

○ Meanwhile, boil the kettle, put the noodles in a heatproof bowl, then pour on boiling water to cover. Leave to sit for 5ish minutes until the noodles are soft, then drain thoroughly.

○ Once the baguettes are cool enough for you to pick them up, cut the loaves lengthways from the front, so they are still held together at the back, and tear out most of the crumb in the centre – you'll need this space in order to fit everything in; makes it a better eat too.

○ Mix the noodles with the do chua, coriander, sugar snaps and spring onions, then dress with the leftover soy-ses sauce.

○ Lightly spread the bottom cavity of each baguette with mayo, then lay down a couple of baby gem leaves, followed by the noodle mix.

○ Finish with mint leaves, a hefty throw of peanuts and a squeeze of lime juice, then get noshing.

AT LEAST A DAY BEFORE

Do do chua

HALF AN HOUR BEFORE

Get your scallops and steaming apparatus ready to the point of putting it on the heat

10 MINUTES TO GO

Heat up soy-ses oil and slice spring onions

5 MINUTES TO GO

Scallops on to steam and finish dish

NEXT DAY

Relax into your banh mi

linguine con gamberino

AROMATIC PRESERVED LEMONS

PREP: 20 MINS • LEAVE: 1 MONTH MINIMUM

MIDDLE-OF-THE-MED PRAWN LINGUINE

PREP: 10 MINS • COOK: 15 MINS

CAPER & OREGANO SALMORIGLIO

PREP: 5 MINS

Having lived with this book for nigh on a year now, it's become clear to me that the threesomes of recipes fall into, you guessed it, three categories. The lion's share is where the slow is the main hoo-ha, the One, the hero of the table. Then there's a second category where our slow isn't the principle on the stage, but has a very necessary supporting role. More than a sidekick, it's the one that allows the star to shine.

But in our final and smallest collective, the Slow is just there for the love of cooking. And this is one of those recipes.

You can buy preserved lemons from most supermarkets or delis these days, so why make them? Well, you either are that kind of person or you're not. It's a bit like why make your own marmalade when there's such a variety of good ones on the shelves. And the only answer I can think of is that it's just not quite the same. Absolutely acceptable – and I'd much rather that you bought your preserved lemons than walked on by this simple summery pasta – but just not quite the dream team.

I've realised by now in my life that I write books that appeal to you folks out there who really do enjoy cooking as much as I do, rather than the have-a-go cook. So go on, I dare you: make my day, go pickle some lemons and next month's prawn linguine will taste all the better for it. Promise.

AROMATIC PRESERVED LEMONS

1kg lemons (small is better for this and the number depends on size, obviously)

2 fresh chillies, left whole (I prefer red, but no biggie)

3 bay leaves

150g sea salt

1 teaspoon coriander seeds

½ teaspoon fennel seeds

* You will also need a 1-litre Kilner jar (other brands are available).

○ First sterilise your jar in whatever way you like: either in a preheated oven at 150°C/130°C fan/gas mark 2 for 10 minutes or by submerging it, plus lid in a bowl of boiling water.

○ Meanwhile, wash the lemons, chillies and bay in cold water and pat dry.

○ Put a third of the lemons to one side, then choose a sharp paring knife and get surgical with the remainder. With the lemon lying flat on your board, imagine you're going to slice it into four long quarters, but you don't actually cut through either end. Start by inserting the knife about 1cm below the stem end and so that it comes out the other side in the same place. Now stand the lemon on its end and bring the knife down to 1cm above the other end. Pull it out, turn the lemon 90 degrees and do the same thing again, so it's still whole with four connected wedges. Now repeat with the others.

○ Gather your ingredients together: split lemons, a pile of weighed-out salt and the aromatics (chillies, bay, corry and fennel seeds).

○ Pick up one of your cut lemons, squeeze the top and bottom, and pack a teaspoon of salt into it via the four slashes, making sure you penetrate all the way to the middle.

○ Drop it into the sterilised jar and chuck a couple of tablespoons of salt plus a few fennel seeds in after it. Do the same with the remainder, bringing some chilli, bay and corry seeds into the equation along the way; by now it should be pretty tightly packed in there.

○ Juice the remaining lemons and pour into the jar. All the lemons need to be submerged, so make sure you really push them down to bring up the level of the liquid, topping up with cold water if necessary (depends on how juicy your lemons are).

○ Seal and keep in a cool, dark place to do their thang for a month.

You won't need to use all of these for the pasta dish over the page, but they last for monthsandmonthsandmonths so just get in the habit of chopping them into grains, salads etc... And may I also direct you to the rather special dressing on page 65?

MIDDLE-OF-THE-MED PRAWN LINGUINE

good slosh of olive oil

300g linguine (fresh, as in supermarket fresh, or dried, which would actually be my preference for this dish)

splash of extra virgin olive oil

30g butter

40g pine nuts

400g raw King prawns (frozen are fine), peeled, deveined and split to the tail, but leave the tail on for pretty

150g cherry tomatoes, halved

2 tablespoons preserved lemons, finely chopped (no pips)

1 x recipe Caper & Oregano Salmoriglio (see below)

80g rocket, very roughly chopped

S & P

Italian in its heart; Moroccan in its demeanour.

○ Put a really big pan of water over a high heat with a good pinch of salt and a fair slosh of olive oil for the pasta – the pan is eventually going to hold all the ingredients, which is why it needs to be a big 'un.

○ Once at a rolling boil, tip the pasta in, stir with tongs to separate and then cook until al dente – usually a minute less than it says on the packet, but you need to try it.

○ Drain into a colander, give it a little splash of extra virgin and shuffle with a fork so it doesn't all stick together, then put the pan straight back on the hob over a medium–high heat.

○ Once the pan is dried, melt the butter in it and as it bubbles and fizzles, throw in the pine nuts. Stir constantly until golden, then add the prawns and carry on moving them around as the prawns start to go pink.

○ Before they are cooked through – about 3 minutes – go in with the cherry toms and preserved lemons and increase the heat to high.

○ Fry it all together until the toms are starting to soften, then turn the heat off and tip in the linguine and salmoriglio.

○ Give it all a damn good mix, season with black pepper only (no salt) and when you're happy with the flavour, stir through the rocket to just wilt.

○ From when the rocket goes in, you want it to be on people's forks in less than a minute. Or something like that.

CAPER & OREGANO SALMORIGLIO

50ml extra virgin olive oil

4 tablespoons (60ml) boiling water

juice of 1 lemon

1 small clove of garlic, finely chopped

a big handful of flat-leaf parsley, chopped

2 tablespoons oregano leaves, picked and roughly chopped (failing that, 1 teaspoon dried – but do try to get fresh, it's worth it)

2 tablespoons capers, small ones left whole or biggies roughly chopped

S & P

○ At a decent pace, whisk the olive oil in a small bowl, then pour in the boiling water in a thin steam, whisking constantly so that it emulsifies.

○ Keep the bicep workout going as you add the lemon juice, again in a thin stream.

○ Once it's all incorporated, stir in the garlic, herbs, capers and seasoning to taste.

MAKES THE RIGHT AMOUNT FOR THE PRAWN LINGUINE

Timeline

A MONTH OR SO BEFORE

Make the preserved lemons

AN HOUR BEFORE

Prep prawns

Knock up the salmoriglio

15 MINUTES BEFORE

Pasta water on, cook and finish dish

chapter seven

mains without a face
(aka veggie mains)

It's telling that when I was at the ideas stage for this chapter, where vegetables are elevated from the usual role of sidekick to Star Turn, my mind mostly drifted to foreign climates and cuisines. In Britain, as is true for the rest of the affluent world, largely speaking a meal isn't considered a proper meal unless it's got something dead in the middle of the table – and preferably one that had blood in its veins.

However, slowly but increasingly we are becoming more aware that meat is not a must, and in fact that the must is that we eat less of it for our planet's sake. There are many countries where for average folks meat is unaffordable day to day so ingredients are simply what you or your neighbours can grow. Their cuisines have evolved to make the most of the fruits of our earth, and as a result have a much more interesting vegetarian repertoire than bacon-bonkers Blighty.

So what follows is one from the Far East, two from the Middle (East), an Indian and a token Brit thrown in for good

measure... which sounds like a bad joke waiting to happen. All of them are proper dinners, some lighter, some more filling, and they all have a naturalness to them that is slightly intangible but nevertheless undeniably present by virtue of being face-free.

To be totally honest, trying to work out how to make the Wonderful World of Veg fit into my commitment to a Slow aspect to the dishes was a bit of a challenge: a couple of the recipes ahead are just regular long and low cooks from the butternut and aubergine collectives, and of course we had to have a pulse-based dish – that overnight soak was too much of a gift of a Slow to walk on by. But then in the interest of thinking outside the usual veg box, we round it all off with some Korean overnight pickles and a quick lesson in how to make your own paneer... because as we all know, Blessed are the Cheese Makers.

party piece baked butternut

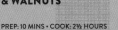

SLOW-ROAST BUTTERNUT
WITH HONEY & WALNUTS

PREP: 10 MINS • COOK: 2½ HOURS

WIN-WIN DOLCELATTE DIP

PREP: 5 MINS

GRILLED PEAR & WATERCRESS SALAD

PREP: 5 MINS • COOK: 6 MINS

In amongst our veggie mains we really wanted to do a party piece spectacular – the soil-dwelling equivalent of a Côte de Boeuf – and what finer, favourite veg was there to do this with than a couple of beautiful, majestic butternuts. And then bringing to mind the recent food trend of salt-baking veg (though the good folks of the Canaries have been doing it with their spuds for centuries), I had a Eureka moment and within a couple of minutes my squash was buried deep in little white rocks. Well, all I can say is there's no need for you to ever try this yourself... one muppet murdering an innocent squash is enough around here.

There are, however, no wasted lessons in cookery, so when I went at it again I made sure that the squash had all the aromatics and seasoning it needed (not to mention giving it a wide open surface so that some of its water content was allowed to evaporate, rather than sadistically forcing it to stew in it) to become the thing of beauty Deniz and I both knew was lurking in there. The studding, glazing and crusting of the butternut rendered just the result I'd had in mind, and with the crisp green-tasting pears and watercress on the side and a hearty splodge of our favourite dolcelatte dip, my dream of the Party Piece Butternut was finally realised.

SLOW-ROAST BUTTERNUT
WITH HONEY & WALNUTS

SERVES 6

2 whole butternut squash (each about 1kg), washed and left unpeeled

4 tablespoons olive oil

8 cloves of garlic, cut into thickish shards (you should get 6–8 matchstick studs out of a fattish clove)

4 tablespoons runny honey

S & P

○ Preheat the oven to 150°C/130°C fan/gas mark 2. For Operation Butternut, you'll need both your biggest and smallest knives (both non-serrated, *s'il vous plait*). Use the big guy to cut each butternut in half lengthways, then scoop the seeds out with a spoon and use the little guy to score the flesh in a cross-hatch, deep enough to really penetrate, but be careful not to go through the skin. Do a few random pokes around the seed cavity too.

○ Move the prepped butternuts into a tight-fitting roasting tray, drizzle over a healthy amount of olive oil, season well with salt and pepper (and I really do mean well – she'll soak it up during cooking and, to be frank, she needs it) and throw them into the middle of the oven for an hour.

CONTINUED ON PAGE 166

Timeline

2 HOURS BEFORE

Get butternut
slow-roasting

Make the breadcrumb
crust and dolcelatte dip

20–25 MINS BEFORE

Crust the butternut and
return to the oven

Get going on the pear
prep and grilling…

…and hopefully it'll all
come together round
about the same time

FOR THE CRUST

130g fresh breadcrumbs

3 stalks of rosemary, leaves picked and finely chopped

70g Parmesan, grated on the small holes

80g walnuts, very roughly chopped

4 tablespoons extra virgin olive oil

2 spring onions, sliced, for scattering at the end

S&P

○ By this time the flesh will have softened enough for you to push the garlic shards into the slashes (doesn't matter if they're sticking out), then spoon over the honey and baste with the juices accumulated in the seed cavity. Stick them back in the oven for a further 45 minutes whilst you get on with making the crust.

○ Spread the breadcrumbs out on a baking tray and pop in the oven under the butternut for 10ish minutes, giving them a shuffle round halfway through – you want them to dry out but not colour. Tip them into a bowl and mix with all the other ingredients (keeping a few walnuts for the end), plus a judicious amount of seasoning.

○ Once the garlic-stabbed butternuts have had their time in the oven, whip them out and turn the oven up to 180°C/160°C fan/gas mark 4.

○ Share the crust between the butternuts, lightly filling the cavities too, then bake for a further 20–25 minutes until they become an inviting golden brown all over.

○ Find a suitably Bacchanalian serving platter and arrange the squishy squashes on it. Generously fill their cavities with cheesy dip, pile the pear and watercress salad high on the side and top it all off with the last of the walnuts.

WIN-WIN DOLCELATTE DIP (See Party Snarfes on page 17)

GRILLED PEAR & WATERCRESS SALAD

FOR 6

3 hard pears (like Conference), skin-on, washed, cored and cut into eighths

1 lemon

3 tablespoons extra virgin olive oil

about 130g (2 supermarket baggies) watercress

1 crisp apple, quartered, cored and thinly sliced

S & P

○ Toss the prepped pears in a bowl with the juice of ½ lemon, a tablespoon of olive oil and some seasoning.

○ Put a griddle pan over a high heat and when it's smoking hot, lay down as many pieces of pear as will fit in one layer – you can pack them pretty closely.

○ Don't fiddle with them for 3ish minutes, then use tongs to lift one up and see if it's got good stripes on it, at which point turn it over and do the same with all of its mates.

○ Cook for the same amount of time on the other side, then taste one: you want it to be cooked on the outside with a bit of bite in the middle. Take them off and put back in the bowl (doesn't matter if they cool as this one isn't temp sensitive) and get on with the next lot.

○ When all the pears are grilled to perfection, toss together with the watercress, sliced apple, remaining lemon juice and olive oil plus seasoning to taste, then cuddle it up next to the baked butternut.

chilli paneer roti

NIGELLA PANEER

PREP: 5 MINS • COOK: 10 MINS • LEAVE: OVERNIGHT

GARLIC ROTI

PREP: 15 MINS • COOK: 2–3 MINS

SAG PANEER

PREP: 5 MINS • COOK: 25 MINS

This is one where I can sense you contemplating walking on by the Slow recipe and purchasing your paneer from the shop, but all I can say is more fool you if you do. Making paneer is simple, satisfying, interesting, quick (it's the time it needs in the fridge to set that defines it as a Slow) and, above all, renders a result far superior to anything you can buy. To the natives of the subcontinent, buying paneer is like us buying French dressing or pre-made mash. You can, but really that says a whole lot about you and not much about your care for good food.

No getting round it, this takes a lot of spinach – four average supermarket bags at 200g each, but it goes to nothing and this is a sag-based dish after all.

Just a lovely, simple recipe, made marvellous with the roti. I was happy with it as soon as it all came together, but it was nice to have that opinion endorsed by the seconds and thirds I found the fine palate of Isabelle Tawil enjoying the next day... and when I nicked a forkful I was amazed how the flavours had come out singing overnight. You know what I'm saying – do the sag paneer the day before for maximum pleasure.

NIGELLA PANEER

MAKES ABOUT 400–500G (ENOUGH FOR 4–6 PORTIONS OF SAG PANEER)

2 litres gold-top milk

1 teaspoon salt

1 teaspoon nigella (black onion) seeds

400g full-fat Greek yogurt

80ml lemon juice (juice from about 2 lemons)

You will also need a piece of muslin about 50cm square.

○ As a bit of *mise en place* for later, line a colander with the muslin so that it's hanging over the edge with about 5cm or so surplus all round, then sit it in the sink.

○ Put the milk, salt and nigella seeds into a heavy-based saucepan over a low–medium heat, stirring it all the time with a spatula to stop it scalding on the bottom.

○ When it gets to steaming (a childhood smell if ever there was one), but before it starts to simmer, spoon the yogurt in, which will start the curdling process.

○ Keep moving it around, systematically sweeping the bottom of the pan so it doesn't stick, and after 5–10 minutes lower in a slotted spoon. Bring it to the surface and you should be looking at something akin to watery cottage cheese.

○ Tip in the lemon juice, stirring all the time as it thickens, then turn the heat off and tip the entire contents of the pan into your prepared muslin-lined colander: it should now look like the worst kind of scrambled eggs – pale and insipid.

○ After a couple of minutes draining time, gather the edges of the muzzy up to make a sac and tie somewhere to hang – I use the arm of the tap overhanging my sink or a suitably arty chair, but whatever works for you.

○ Once cool enough to handle, give it a good squeeze, then leave for an hour or so to drip-dry, giving the sac a massaging grope every now and then.

○ When it's firm to touch and no more liquid is coming out of it, give it a final throttling squeeze to get out any lingering water (essential or it won't fry properly) then wrap it tightly in clingfilm, muzzy and all, and put in the fridge to set overnight.

GARLIC ROTI (See Mutton Madras on page 61)

SAG PANEER

800g fresh whole leaf spinach (preferably not baby, but it'll do)

2 tablespoons plain oil (such as vegetable)

2 tablespoons butter

1 large or 2 small onions, sliced

3–4 cloves of garlic, chopped

1–2 regular green chillies (or use bird's eye if you really want to blow it up), sliced and seeds left in

20g fresh ginger, washed, trimmed and grated on the big holes

½ teaspoon garam masala

½ teaspoon ground turmeric

150g cherry tomatoes

1 x recipe Nigella Paneer (see opposite), muslin peeled off and cut into rough 3–4cm dice

juice of ½ lemon

couple of hefty splodges of yogurt (around 4 tablespoons), to serve (recommended, but deeply optional)

S & P

○ First up, put a big pan of water over a high heat with a couple of healthy pinches of salt. Whilst it comes to a rolling boil, you might as well get on with some veg prep (chopping your onions, garlic, chillies, ginger).

○ When the water is up to speed, chuck the spinach in there a handful at a time, using a slotted spoon to press each load beneath the surface of the water.

○ Once all the spinach is in there (doesn't matter if the pan is full to busting), tip it into a colander and run under cold water to cool.

○ Pick up a handful and squeeze all the water out of it, then put it aside and do the same with the rest. Roughly chop the spinach balls and now you're ready to get going in earnest.

○ Heat the oil in your widest decent pan and, once it's good and hot (but not explosive), gently lay in the paneer pieces. Fry for 2–3 minutes until golden brown on the bottom, then turn. Once they've reached a similarly pleasing hue on the other side, lift them out and put aside to degrease on kitchen roll.

○ Lower the heat slightly, then melt the butter in the oil and, once it's fizzling away, fry the onion until it starts to soften.

○ Stir in the garlic, chilli, ginger and ground spices and keep it fizzling away like this for a good 5ish minutes.

○ Add the chopped spinach, cherry toms and half a mug of water. Stir well to coat, then put a lid on and cook for another 10–15 minutes until the tomatoes are bursting and the spinach has lost its bright greenness, settling into a more appropriate muted shade.

○ Fold in the fried paneer and once it's warmed through, turn the heat off and finish with lemon juice and seasoning.

○ Now's the time to stir through the yoggy if you fancy it, which I rather do having tried it with and without... but that's entirely your call.

Timeline

DAY/2 DAYS BEFORE

Make, drain and wrap the paneer

ANYTIME UP TO 30 MINUTES BEFORE

Put water on for spinach-blanching

Make the roti dough (but don't roll yet)

Follow sag recipe and once spinach and toms are in, put griddle on

Roll out roti and cook

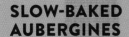

SLOW-BAKED AUBERGINES

PREP: 5 MINS • COOK: 2 HOURS

POMEGRANOUSH

PREP: 5 MINS

PALAK BAIGAN (THE SPINACHY ONE)

PREP: 5 MINS • COOK: 15 MINS

MIRZA GHAZEMI (THE PERSIAN EGGY ONE)

PREP: 5 MINS • COOK: 15 MINS

3-way obo dip

So once again we've departed from our prescribed Quick Quick Slow formula and gone freestyle... always to be encouraged. The aubergine is a mighty beautiful thing. Its slow-baked flesh has a fabulous, unique flavour and texture (I'm steering clear of 'meaty' as that might be considered patronising to our non-flesh noshing friends), which is why it's so important and popular in vegetarian cookery.

Back in the room, or rather the oven, our Slow is three skin-shrivelled long-baked obos, squishy to the point of collapse, and frankly looking externally nothing like the goodies they hold inside.

And it's those goodies that are our Quicks: each obo is peeled, chopped and sent in a different direction to make three very different but compatible dips, one from Iran (Mirza Ghazemi), another from India (Palak Baigan), and lastly a slightly itinerant Pomegranoush (like a Baba with pom tendencies) from somewhere around the eastern shore of the Med.

They're great on their own but interesting to compare as a threesome, as it really shows off the versatility of these big black mamas.

SLOW-BAKED AUBERGINES

3 large/6 small aubergines

3 cloves of garlic, unpeeled

khobez flatbread, warmed, to serve

- ❍ Preheat the oven to 140°C/120°C fan/gas mark 1 and poke the aubergines all over with a fork.

- ❍ Pop them onto a baking tray with the garlic and bake low and slow for 2 hours, taking the garlic out after an hour.

- ❍ Leave to cool, then cut the top off each one, peel off the puckered skin and prepare for your 3-way...

POMEGRANOUSH

FOR THE DIP

⅓ of the Slow-baked Aubergines
(see opposite, which may be 1 or
2 depending on size), peeled

3 roasted cloves of garlic, peeled
(the ones that went in with the
aubergines)

2 tablespoons Greek yogurt

zest and juice of ½ lemon

2 tablespoons tahini

2 teaspoons pomegranate
molasses, plus more to taste

S & P

TO FINISH

a handful of flat-leaf parsley,
chopped

a handful of pomegranate seeds
(half a pom)

a bit of extra virgin olive oil

- ○ Put the aubergine in a food processor with all the
  other dip ingredients.

- ○ Pulse until roughly smooth, then taste for
  seasoning.

- ○ Scrape into a pretty bowl and finish with chopped
  parsley, pom seeds and a good glug of olive oil.

Timeline

Obv bake the obos
first, then it's kind of
anywayyouwanna...
but if it were me I'd
do the Pomegranoush
first, then the Spinachy
one and finish up on
the Persian guy as it's
soooo yummy straight
from the pan

MIRZA GHAZEMI (THE PERSIAN EGGY ONE)

2 tablespoons olive oil

1 small white onion, thinly sliced

1 clove of garlic, minced

¼ teaspoon ground turmeric

1 teaspoon tomato purée

2 vine-ripened plum tomatoes,
roughly diced

⅓ Slow-baked Aubergines (see
opposite, which may be 1 or 2
depending on size), peeled and
finely chopped/blitzed in a food
processor

1 egg, beaten

S & P

- ○ Warm the oil in a saucepan over a low–medium heat and sauté the
  onion and garlic until soft and sweet – about 6–8 minutes.

- ○ Stir in the turmeric to coat, then carry on cooking gently as you
  splodge in the tomato purée.

- ○ Keep stirring to stop the purée from sticking to the bottom, and give it
  a couple of minutes of lethargic fizzling before you tip in the toms.

- ○ Hold the tempo as it is and once the tomatoes have started to soften
  and are less watery, add the mushy aubergine flesh.

- ○ Turn the heat up to medium, mix well and when the toms are as
  squidgy as the aubergines – about another 3ish minutes – grab
  yourself a spatula, pour the egg into the pan and beat quickly until
  amalgamated and you can't see any strands of egg.

- ○ Give it a good old season and tuck in straightaway – it's best eaten
  immediately, but it's also bloody delicious cold from the fridge
  for brekkie.

PALAK BAIGAN (THE SPINACHY ONE)

1 onion, chopped

3 cloves of garlic, chopped

2 tablespoons olive oil

3 cardamom pods

¼ teaspoon ground cumin

⅓ Slow-baked Aubergines, (see page 174, which may be 1 or 2 depending on size) peeled and roughly chopped

500g fresh whole leaf spinach, roughly chopped

zest and juice of 1 lemon

½ teaspoon nigella (black onion) seeds, plus a smattering at the end for prettiness

slosh of extra virgin olive oil

S & P

lemon wedges and a few blobs of Greek yogurt, to serve

○ Gently fry the onion and garlic in the oil, without colouring, until softened and sweetening – about 5 minutes.

○ Crush the cardamom pods with the side of a chef's knife, then pick out the seeds and discard the pods.

○ Stir in the cardamom seeds and cumin, reduce the heat and continue to cook oh-so-gently for another 5 minutes or so.

○ Now increase the heat to high and use a spatula to turn through the naked, chopped aubergine flesh so that it's completely saturated in the spiced oil, squishing it to break it up as you go.

○ When it's well combined and piping hot, add the spinach, a handful at a time, stirring constantly so that as soon as each handful wilts it becomes a part of the mix.

○ Once all the spinach is in the pan and wilted, keep stirring over a high heat until all the water has come out of it and the contents of the pan are starting to stick to the bottom.

○ Turn off the heat, stir in the lemon zest and juice (probably about ½ lemon) and a good amount S & P to taste. Leave to cool a bit before sliding it into a bowl and finishing with a scattering of nigella seeds, a few blobs of yogurt, a slosh of extra virgin and some lemons on the side.

dong dang summer rolls

SUMMER ROLLS

LEAVE: OVERNIGHT • PREP: 10 MINS • COOK: 6 MINS

SRIRACHA DIPPING SAUCE

COOK: 3–5 MINS

DO CHUA (VIETNAMESE PICKLES)

PREP: 15 MINS • LEAVE: OVERNIGHT

BLACKENED TENDERSTEM
WITH SESAME & GARLIC

PREP: 5 MINS • COOK: 10 MINS

I remember my first summer roll: 1995. It was my first New York summer as a chef and a friend took me to a Vietnamese restaurant (a cuisine yet to hit London) in Chinatown. In the high heat of the day, I fell instantly for their cool crunchiness – sooo superior to the deep-fried rolls it seems totally wrong to associate with the freshness of spring.

Having said many a time in both this book and others, although my recipes are a bit of a run around the world, I like to stay true to one kind of cuisine within each particular dish.

Well, as I also say both in this book and others, Rules are there to be Broken. These three recipes are a veritable visa-toting, border-crossing, all-singing, all-dancing Asian circus; the raw rolls themselves are, in essence, Vietnamese and contain my current fave pickle mix from that country, Do Chua. Tofu has, I believe, been embraced by most South East Asian countries, but by all accounts was invented by the Chinese around the time of Christ; and with the five-spice blend in the marinade completes the Sino aspect of our dish. And then we have a dipping sauce based on Thailand's hottest condiment, both in terms of chilli and now as an annoyingly on-trend ingredient: sriracha.

I needed a name for this travelling trio, and coming from a family where maps were read like bedtime stories (that's what happens if you have an historian/cartographer father), I looked on the map and there it was, right on the Viet-China border: Dong Dang. (Sorry Thailand, but there is no place where all three countries share a border, and arguably yours is the most replaceable ingredient on the table.)

Bingo! Or rather as Terry Thomas used to say, 'Ding Dong'!

NB: It really has to be firm tofu or else it's a bit of a nightmare… believe me I've tried. You should be able to get it in your supermarket, but if you've an Asian shop near you I'd bother making the trip not only for the tofu but for some of the other ingredients too – better quality for sure.

Timeline

DAY BEFORE

Knock up the pickles and marinate the tofu

AN HOUR BEFORE KICK-OFF

Drain and fry the tofu

Make the Sriracha dipping sauce (toasting enough sesame seeds for the broccoli recipe too)

Prep the spring onions and herbs

30 MINS BEFORE THE WHISTLE

Heat up griddle

Griddle broccoli >> toss and dress

Soak wrappers >> start making wraps

DO CHUA (VIETNAMESE PICKLES)

(See Steamed Scallops with Do Chua on page 154)

SRIRACHA DIPPING SAUCE

MAKES ENOUGH FOR
4 SHALLOW SAUCERS

1 tablespoon sesame seeds

4 tablespoons rice wine vinegar

1–2 teaspoons sriracha, depending on how hot you can take it (it's pretty fiery with just one)

2 tablespoons light soy sauce

1 spring onion, green part only, very thinly sliced (keep the whites for the summer rolls)

○ Toast the sesame seeds in a small, dry pan over a low–medium heat for 3–5 minutes, tossing regularly until they have moved from beige to golden brown.

○ In a small bowl, stir together the vinegar, sriracha and soy.

○ Pour into four shallow saucers (or whatever you have knocking around), then float the sesame seeds and spring onions on top.

DONG DANG SUMMER ROLLS

MAKES 12 WRAPS (2 EACH AS A STARTER FOR 6, 3 EACH AS A MAIN FOR 4, OR GREAT FOR PARTY NIBBLES)

1 block firm tofu (usually around 300–350g)

12 rice wrappers

FOR THE TOFU MARINADE

4 decent cloves of garlic (15g), minced

40g fresh ginger, washed, knobbly bits trimmed off, then finely grated (microplane ideal)

100ml dark soy sauce

4 tablespoons sweet chilli sauce

zest of 2 limes and juice of 1 (the other being for your G & T)

½ teaspoon Chinese five-spice

FOR THE FILLING

a big handful of mint leaves

a big handful of coriander (stalks and all)

4 spring onions, thinly sliced on an angle

2 tablespoons peanut or vegetable oil

½ recipe Do Chua (see page 154), squeezed dry (the other half is for the next time you make this or for the great Banh Mi on page 157)

* You'll also need two clean tea towels: one dry, one damp.

○ Slice the block of tofu into three long Stongehenge-like slabs, then cut each one into four, so you have 12 sticks.

○ Locate a suitable vessel to hold them in a fairly close-packed way (a Tupperware moment perhaps), then mix all the ingredients for the marinade in it.

○ Now lay in the tofu fingers and gently give them a roll around to coat on all sides... and if at this stage you can leave to marinade for oh, let's say overnight, then that's nothing but a good thing.

○ When you're about an hour from serving, prep the herbs and spring onions for the rolls, and put a wide frying pan on the stove with enough oil to cover the bottom of it.

○ Once the oil is really jolly hot, lay half the tofu sticks in and fry for around 3 minutes a side until through the golden to lightly blackened stage. Take out and lay on kitchen paper as you do the next batch.

○ When all the tofu is cooked, half-fill a big mixing bowl with hot water and spread the dry tea towel out in front of you.

○ In quick succession, frisbee three rice wrappers into the hot water, pushing them down under the surface of the water: watch as they turn white and opaque – just a couple of minutes, which is just the time you need to arrange all the filling ingredients around you.

○ The wrappers are pretty fragile now, so one by one, carefully lift them out with your hands and spread out in a row on the dry tea towel.

○ Quickly load them up with some of the Do Chua, tofu, herbs and spring onions (the tenderstem can go in too, or on the side, or both), then give them a good tight roll – the wraps are helpfully sticky now, so believe me when I say it's easier done than said.

○ When these three are ready, put them aside, drape the damp tea towel over them and off you go again. Fun and games!

○ And when it comes to serving, you may want to cut them in half on an angle to show off their pretty insides...

BLACKENED TENDERSTEM
WITH SESAME & GARLIC (see Squid with Szechuan Mayo & Blackened Tenderstem on page 140)

lazy turkish beans

BARBUNYA PILAKI (AKA 'GRANDMOTHER'S BEANS')

SOAK: OVERNIGHT · PREP: 10 MINS · COOK: 2½ HOURS · LEAVE: 1–2 DAYS

THYME FLATBREADS

PREP: 2 HOURS · COOK: 5 MINS

BANGING EGG BREKKIE

PREP: 5 MINS · COOK: 10 MINS

Over the years, I've done pretty much everything you can with a pulse (as it were), including having the fire brigade called to my school as a six-year-old for shoving a mung bean too far up my nose (and no, I've never quite understood why it was the fire brigade either).

So when I saw we needed a bean-based recipe in this chapter, I threw it over to my now-familiar co-cook on this book, Turkish Deniz… and enter Barbunya Pilaki.

To Turks this is like your mum's shepherd's pie, or hotpot or crumble; it's the one you dream about when you miss home, and plead that she makes on your return.

It's a simple mezze, usually served up with fish or kofte as part of a spread, and having had it a few times now I can see how it finds a way into your heart.

Two things you need to know to enjoy your Barbunya Pilaki (literally 'stewing beans' – yum!) to the max: firstly, sorry, but you really do need to let them sit for a day or two, otherwise you just won't get the golden moment. And secondly, don't overheat them – they're best at room temp (and by that imagine a room on the Aegean coast, where this dish comes from, so maybe put them in the airing cupboard or a low oven for a bit).

As far as the flatbread goes, although it's quick to cook it does need time to prove, which makes this set more Slow Slow Quick than Quick Quick Slow – more rule breaking… sigh.

Deniz says that you have to drink raki with it – she said it three times so it must be important – which seems like the perfect moment to bring up the Banging Egg Brekkie; what leftovers – and hangovers – are made for.

I love it when a plan comes together.

Timeline

2–3 DAYS BEFORE
Soak beans

1–2 DAYS BEFORE
Simmer then braise beans in oven>>cool

2 HOURS BEFORE SERVING
Knock-up flatbread and prove

AS BEAN TIME APPROACHES
Warm them through; roll and cook flatbreads

NEXT MORNING
I like my eggs banging pls

BARBUNYA PILAKI
(AKA 'GRANDMOTHER'S BEANS', A FIGURATIVE TRANSLATION, NOT A LITERAL ONE)

FOR 4, WITH THE FLATBREADS AND ANOTHER COUPLE OF MEZZE (LIKE THE TURKEY BURGERS ON PAGE 24 AND ANY OF THE AUBERGINE DIPS ON PAGE 172–176) PLUS ENOUGH LEFTOVERS FOR 2 FOLKS TO ENJOY THE BANGING EGG BREKKIE

150g dried borlotti or pinto beans

150g dried haricot beans

some assorted aromatics for the bean cooking water (any combo of the following: onion, peeled and halved; carrot, peeled; celery, tomato, thyme, bay, garlic)

4 tablespoons olive oil

1 large onion, diced

1 large carrot, cut into rough 2cm dice

1 large potato, peeled and cut into 4cm cubes

1 teaspoon paprika

400g tin chopped tomatoes

1 teaspoon caster sugar

couple of bay leaves

S & P

TO SERVE

more olive oil (or even better, extra virgin)

a big handful of chopped parsley

lemon wedges

strained yogurt (optional), though Deniz says her Turkish Nene (Granny to you and me) Zehra, would deeply disapprove

○ Soak the beans together overnight in cold water – this not only softens them, but also helps to reduce their methane characteristic.

○ The next day, drain and rinse the beans, then tip into a standard ovenproof casseroling pan big enough to hold all the ingredients. Chuck in whatever combo of the aromatics you have knocking around (the more the merrier) and cover with cold water.

○ Pop a lid on, bring to the boil, then reduce the heat and simmer until the beans begin to soften, topping them up with water as and when so they are just covered. They could take anywhere from 40 minutes to 1½ hours... a big window, I know, but that's beans for you: fabulous but unreliable. The haricots will be ready before the borlotti/pinto (who will never become as tender due to their chalky nature) but no matter, just keep going until the bigger guys are beginning to soften.

○ Drain over a bowl, keeping the murky but flavoursome water, then pick out and chuck the aromatics.

○ Preheat the oven to 160°C/140°C fan/gas mark 3. Give the pan a quick clean, then put it back on a medium heat and pour in the oil. Once it's hot, sauté the onion for a good few minutes until starting to soften.

○ Tip in the carrot, potato and paprika, then stir to coat for another minute or so before chucking everybody else in there: tin of toms, sugar, bay and beans as well as a mug of the bean cooking water and a decent effort on the seasoning front.

○ Pop the lid on, bring to the boil, then put in the oven for 1¾ hours, giving it a quick stir halfway through if you're in the area (no biggie if you're not) – you're waiting for everything to soften and come together in a lazy way.

○ Leave to cool, and preferably let it sit overnight (or for two nights), but any which way, this is one to be enjoyed at my favourite temperature for food i.e. warm armpit – you may want to add a splash of water when you reheat as the beans tend to soak up the juice. Have a last seasoning check, then finish with a generous flourish of good oil, chopped parsley and lemon wedges to squeeze over. And Deniz's Granny is right – it really doesn't need the yoggy... but I still like it!

THYME FLATBREADS
(See McTurcos on page 22, ignoring the bit where it says to 'drape a tea towel over them whilst you are cooking the burgers'. Obviously we're not making burgers here, so just crack on with cooking them straight away.)

BANGING EGG BREKKIE

1 small onion, sliced

2 tablespoons olive oil

about 100g baby spinach

small bowlful (350–400g) of
    Barbunya Pilaki (see opposite)

4 eggs

S & P

TO SERVE

some kind of bread (flatbread –
    ideally the thyme ones if you've
    got any left – or a corn or flour
    tortilla, or just good ole toast)

a handful of coriander, chopped

chilli sauce (sriracha's hard to
    beat)

○ Preheat your grill to hot. In a heavy-based frying
pan, sauté the onion in the oil for a few minutes until
it softens.

○ Stir in the spinach and cook until it has wilted and all
the water has evaporated, then tip in the beans and
season as they warm through.

○ Make four small egg-sized craters in the mix and
crack an egg into each one.

○ Carry on cooking on the stove for a couple of minutes
over a low–medium heat, then stick it under the grill
to set the top of the whites.

○ Finish your banging brekkie with coriander, some
chilli sauce, and... get in!

chapter eight
pudding

When I came up with the overarching concept of a book that married the sublime beauty of taking it slow with a couple of fast and snappy recipes to support and enhance, it's fair to say that the sweet section was not uppermost in my mind.

But when I realised that I had to have a pudding chapter, I threw myself at it with gusto, and by that I mean leant heavily on Deniz, my co-pilot on this book – a woman who has not blood but crème pat in her veins – as well as other mates I may or may not have had the decency to name-check.

And what we've ended up with is a really rather splendid bunch: we may have erred slightly from the devout formula of Quick Quick Slow at some points (or actually to be fair, I don't think any of them exactly follow the prescribed format... no change there), but as a whole, they have character, style and a variety of tempos: above all they are obscenely noshable, slightly spectacular and irreverently fun.

So without trying to get myself off the hook, I think that when all's said and done – and it is now, as this is the last chapter – that really pretty well sums up what I wanted from this book.

Huzzah!

fruity french toast with calvados semifreddo

CALVADOS SEMIFREDDO

PREP: 30 MINS • LEAVE: OVERNIGHT

SUBTLE & SUPPORTIVE POACHED FRUITS

PREP: 3 MINS • COOK: 5-10 MINS

FRENCH TOAST/EGGY BREAD/PAIN PERDU

PREP: 5 MINS • COOK: 10 MINS

Gosh if only all of life were this easy. Spectacular result without need nor reason to ever break into a sweat.

The Semifreddo is a done deal once you've got all the air into it that our atmosphere can spare, and sometime before pudding is even on the horizon, the poached fruits can be brought to fruition and then left aside to rest. (I've set out three seasonal alternatives to give you the general idea, then after that just run with whatever you fancy.)

The only time the pace ramps up at all is on the home straight: don't rush for the line though, as before you soak the brioche, your Semifreddo needs to be slightly soft to the touch i.e. not rock hard, and the poached fruits warmed on the hob.

But there is one thing that has continually bothered me about this near perfect recipe: is it French Toast, Eggy Bread or Pain Perdu???

CALVADOS SEMIFREDDO

300ml double cream

½ teaspoon vanilla extract

100g caster sugar

4 eggs, separated

3 tablespoons Calvados (or if you're on a budget buy a brandy miniature)

MAKES 1 LOAF (ABOUT 8 GOOD SLICES, BUT BOTH THE QUICKS SERVE 6, SO IN THEORY THAT LEAVES YOU A COUPLE OF SLICES FOR ANOTHER HAPPY DAY)

○ Line a 20 x 10 x 6cm loaf tin with enough clingfilm so that it hangs over the sides roughly 10cm in all directions.

○ Have your best three mixing bowls to hand: a winning semifreddo is all about aeration... and if you haven't got a stand mixer, mentally prepare yourself for a bit of a work-out – not one for the faint-wristed, as my friend Rachel would say.

○ In the first bowl, whisk the cream and vanilla through the soft peak stage, but stopping short of hard peaks (precise, I know, but you'll recognise the moment when you come upon it).

○ Here's some info about what you're looking for in bowl two: if you have a stand mixer, opt for that, and if not, make it the biggest bowl in the house as it will be the one that everything ends up in. Tip in all but a tablespoon of the sugar, along with the egg yolks and Calvados. Either by hand or by the power of electricity, whisk until the mix has turned thick and pale (we all know someone like that) – called the ribbon stage, and is identifiable by the mixture leaving a trail when you lift up the whisk, and the consistency as it falls off the whisk looking, well, ribbony.

○ The last bowl is for the egg whites (if you've got a stand mixer and are feeling smart/lazy, then move the yolk mix somewhere else, give the bowl a really good clean to degrease or else the whites won't fluff and go in again). Add the remaining tablespoon of sugar and whisk until stiff peaks form, like a meringue. All your ingredients are now ready.

○ Now using a wide spatula, gently fold the cream into the yolk mixture in two to three stages, then do the same with the meringue.

○ Pour into the prepared loaf tin and wrap the clingfilm over the top so it's all enclosed and won't get frostbite.

○ Stick in the freezer overnight; it'll set rock solid so you must take it out about 30 minutes before serving or else it won't soften enough to be a true semifreddo... it'll just be freddo.

Timeline

ANYTIME UP TO A WEEK OR SO PREVIOUS:

Make the semifreddo

ANYTIME UP TO AN HOUR OR SO BEFORE

Poach the fruits

ONCE THEY'RE CLAMOURING FOR PUD

Time for French toast

SUBTLE & SUPPORTIVE POACHED FRUITS

FOR 6

Small disclaimer before you launch into poaching: nature gives us different sizes and varieties of all our fruits, and by the time they get to us they are of different ages (since picked) and ripeness. All of these variables make it hard for me to give you accurate sugar weights and poaching times, and so you really will just have to suck it (and poke it) and see.

PEARS

around 150g caster sugar

3 pears (ideally tall and hardish like Conference, but if you can only get little guys use 4), peeled, cored and sliced into slivers/ shards

½ teaspoon vanilla extract

- Pour the sugar and 300ml water into a saucepan and stir to make a stock syrup – no need to heat at this stage.

- Drop in the pears and vanilla, then bring to a light simmer for roughly 5–10 minutes (depending on variety and ripeness) until they are tender but still with a bit of bite.

- Turn the heat off, but keep the pears in the syrup until you need them.

- When it comes to serving, warm them through, then lift the pears out with a slotted spoon and put straight onto the Semifreddo, which in turn is on the French toast.

PEACHES

6 peaches (not stupidly ripe), halved, stoned and cut into sixths

about 40g caster sugar

½ teaspoon vanilla extract

- Put the peach pieces into the pan with the sugar, vanilla and 50ml water (3 tablespoons plus a little spillage).

- Stick over a medium heat with the lid on and give them the odd swirl over the 4–6 minutes it takes them to poach to perfection. Follow the instructions for pears as to how to finish the job.

PLUMS

These need less water than pears as they release it as they cook. Plums can be a bit tricky to stone, so you can cook them stone-in and pick them out after, which is easier but not as pretty.

4 large/6 regular plums, hard not ripe, halved and stoned, cut into quarters if they're biggies

about 40g caster sugar

½ teaspoon vanilla extract

- Closely pack the plum halves, cut-side up, in a single layer in a saucepan or frying pan.

- Sprinkle on the sugar and vanilla, then pour on 100ml water.

- Set over a low heat with the lid on and gently poach for roughly 5–10 minutes, depending on size, turning them over about halfway through cooking.

- They're ready when a knife goes into them without resistance, then follow the instructions for pears as to how to finish the job.

FRENCH TOAST/EGGY BREAD/ PAIN PERDU

3 eggs
250ml whole milk
pinch of salt
350–400g loaf of brioche
40g butter

○ Preheat the oven to 150°C/130°C fan/gas mark 2 and put a small baking tray plus your pudding plates/bowls in there to warm through.

○ Whisk together the eggs, milk and salt in a bowl and then pour into a roasting tray.

○ Cut the ends off the loaf (keep for toast tomorrow), then slice into six and lay them in the eggy milk.

○ Put your best heavy-based pan on the hob over a medium heat – it's unlikely to be big enough to take all six slices, but ideally it'll hold three at a time with a bit of squishing.

○ After just a couple of minutes, turn the brioche slices over to soak on the other side; you need to keep a bit of a timeline on this... if they over-soak, they'll fall apart as brioche doesn't have much structure.

○ Melt half the butter in the pan and once it's fizzling, swirl it around, then lay in the first three slices (or if you have a ginormous pan like me, then put all the butter in now). Cook for 3ish minutes until golden and browning, then turn over and fry for the same amount of time on the other side.

○ Move this lot onto the warmed baking tray in the oven, chuck the remainder of the butter into the pan and get going on batch two.

○ When you're ready to go, put the French toast onto the warmed dishes, squiffily top with a generous slice of semifreddo, then use a slotted spoon to finish with poached fruit. (You don't want to use much of the poaching liquor, just a bit drizzled around the plate, as too much will make the bread soggy, but once cooled, bottle it and keep for future fun times, like other puds, homemade lemonade, cocktails or next time's poached fruits. Too good to lose and lasts for months in the fridge.)

boozy prune espresso torte

BOOZY PRUNES

PREP: 5–10 MINS • LEAVE: 1 WEEK (OR 1 MONTH)

ESPRESSO TORTE

PREP: 30 MINS • COOK 1¼ HOURS
• LEAVE: OVERNIGHT (AT LEAST)

AMBER AMARETTI CRACKLE

PREP: 5 MINS • COOK 10 MINS • LEAVE: TO COOL

Some time ago I found myself about to give a class at Richard Bertinet's famed cookery school in Bath, and when Richard offered me his go-to for Dutch courage (an espresso with 'a hidden gem'), I didn't hesitate. Well, the hidden gem turned out to be an Agen prune soaked for a month in brandy, and my class turned out to be quite a laugh.

Needless to say it was sufficiently memorable – the coffee combo, not the class – that after a two-year incubation period in my head, it morphed into this super-rich and rather grown-up-tasting torte. Flourless too. Oooo...

 ## BOOZY PRUNES

MAKES ENOUGH FOR ONE KNOCK-OUT TORTE

120g prunes (stoned weight)

70ml brandy

20g caster sugar

○ First sterilise your jar by filling it with boiling water for a minute, then tipping it out and leaving to steam dry.

○ Now put all the ingredients into the jar, then give it a good shake every now and then over 5–10 minutes to dissolve the sugar, until you can't see any granules settled on the bottom.

○ Squish the prunes down below the surface of the liquid, then put the lid on and leave at room temp for a week... or a month... or a season.

BOOZY PRUNE ESPRESSO TORTE

FOR 8 LUCKY PEOPLE

175g 70% dark chocolate

125g caster sugar

125g salted butter (ideally at room temp), diced, plus a bit more for greasing the tin

1 espresso, or 3 tablespoons of the strongest coffee you can make

100ml hot water

1 x recipe Boozy Prunes (see page 190)

3 eggs, separated

TO FINISH

120g crème fraîche

1 x recipe Amber Amaretti Crackle (opposite)

You'll also need a cake tin 20cm in diameter and 4cm deep.

○ Preheat the oven to 150°C/130°C fan/gas mark 2. Grease the tin with butter, then line with greaseproof paper on the bottom and up the sides so that the paper comes a good few centimetres above the tin (do this using just one piece of paper so you can use it later to lift out the torte... bit fiddly but, having tried it a bunch of ways, I can assure you that this little bit of faff now makes for Big Easy later).

○ Roughly chop the chocolate into smallish pieces, tip into a medium-sized heatproof bowl, then mix with the sugar (keeping a tablespoon aside), butter, espresso and hot water.

○ Choose a saucepan to be the bottom of your bain marie and put about 5cm water in it, making sure that it's not in contact with the bottom of the bowl. Bring to a gentle simmer and keep stirring until the chocolate and butter are fully melted, then take the bowl off and leave to cool to blood temperature (i.e. when you stick the tip of your finger in, it feels neither hot nor cold).

○ Meanwhile, strain the prunes, leaving the boozy syrup to one side, and blitz to a paste in a food-processor.

○ Once the chocolate is sufficiently cool, whisk in the prune purée and egg yolks until fully incorporated.

○ Either in a stand mixer or with beaters, or by hand, whisk the egg whites at a medium speed until they start to foam, then tip in the reserved tablespoon of sugar. Increase the speed until you have reached the glossy stiff peak stage, then using a wide rubber spatula, fold this lightly into the chocolate in three batches. At the end it should have a rich, mousse-like texture with no trails of white. Fill the kettle and stick it on.

○ Scrape the mix into the prepped cake tin, sit it in a roasting tray and pour in boiling water from the kettle to come halfway up the side of the tin.

○ Bake in the middle of the oven for 1¼ hours, at which point your torte should have doubled in volume, be set at the sides but have a slight jiggle to it – there is no point doing the skewer test as you want it to still be gooey inside. Leave to sit in the water for 10 minutes, then lift it out and cool to room temp in the tin: as it cools, it may develop some cracks and crevices on top. If it doesn't, use a toothpick to poke a load of holes all over it – and slowly pour the boozy prune syrup into the cracks (or holes) until the torte has absorbed all the goodness. Cover with clingfilm, stick in the fridge and leave overnight, better still, over two or three nights.

○ When you're an hour or so from pudding, take the torte out of the fridge, tug on the greaseproof to lift it out of the tin, move it onto a serving plate and leave to come up to room temp. When the time is upon you, spread the top with crème fraîche and as a last job (so it stays crunchy) scatter with half the amaretti crackle, spooning the remainder in little piles on the side of each plate.

AMBER AMARETTI CRACKLE

MAKES ENOUGH TO COVER THE TOP OF THE TORTE, PLUS A MINI SAND DUNE ALONGSIDE EACH PLATED SLICE

125g caster sugar

50ml water

50g amaretti biscuits

○ Line a small baking tray with greaseproof paper. For the caramel, choose your favourite heavy-based saucepan and make sure it's really clean (caramel is a volatile beast and hates impurities or foreign bodies).

○ Pour the sugar and water into the pan, then stir with a (clean!) finger until wetted. Put on a high heat and bring to the boil – DO NOT WALK AWAY!!

○ After a while, you'll see that one particular spot is starting to go golden, so give the pan a gentle swirl to dissipate the darker area and even out the heat, but DO NOT STIR! (If the sugar starts to crystallise and solidify on the sides/edges of the pan, dip a pastry brush into a mug of cold water and use to brush down the sides of the pan around that area – taking care not to get the brush in the caramel – which should hopefully break up the crystals.)

○ What you're looking for is an even reddish golden brown – easiest identified with a sugar thermometer as the 'hard-crack stage' (149–154°C). If you don't have a sugar thermometer, watch closely as the bubbles start to get slower and bigger and the caramel begins to darken.

○ As soon as you see the colour change happening it all moves quite quickly: keep swirling the pan to even out the hue. If you are working with a thermometer, take the pan off the heat as soon as the temp hits 145°C, which allows for the temperature of the mix to keep going up a bit once the pan is off the heat – and if not, just look out for an amber-golden colour.

○ Pour immediately into the prepared baking tray and leave to cool until completely hard.

○ Once the caramel is cool and hard, break it up into pieces and put in a food processor. Pulse until you are looking at caramel dust with small bite-sized pieces in there too.

○ Chuck in the amaretti biscuits and whizz briefly again to jewel-like crunchy, amber sand. Keep in an airtight container until needed.

A tip to clean your pan: fill it with water, put it back on the stove and bring to a simmer (with the sugar thermometer in it if you were using one). This will make the caramel dissolve and you just pour it away; otherwise it's a bitch-load of scrubbing.

Timeline

ANYTIME YOU HAVE 5 MINUTES IN YOUR LIFE (UP TO A WEEK BEFORE TORTE-TIME)

Soak the prunes

ONE OR TWO DAYS BEFORE LA GRAND BOUCHE

Make the torte

ANYTIME ON THE DAY

Knock up the crackle

AN HOUR OR SO BEFORE

Take the torte out to come up to room temp

JUST BEFORE SERVING

Crème fraîche the top and sprinkle with dust – Show Time!

SEA SALT MERINGUES

PREP: 20 MINS • COOK 1½ HOURS
• LEAVE: OVERNIGHT

SIMPLE TOFFEE SAUCE

COOK 10 MINS • LEAVE: TO COOL

BISCUITY CHANTILLY

PREP: 10 MINS

salted caramel banoffee mess

This recipe might as well read, 'Take two top puds (banoffee pie and Eton mess) and stick them together using a current food trend'.

Salted caramel goes in the same bag as kale, pulled pork and quinoa. I am well and truly O-ver them and their bad-ass ubiquitous selves. But of course, having said that, there's a reason they've gone stratospheric… and that salt 'n' sweet thing really does work.

This couldn't be simpler, just do the whipped cream and assembly part right at the lastest, as you don't want the bickie bits to go soggy, and frankly it ain't happy hangin' in the fridge.

SEA SALT MERINGUES

2 egg whites, at room temperature

120g caster sugar

1 heaped teaspoon sea salt

○ Preheat the oven to 150°C/130°C fan/gas mark 2, line a large baking tray with greaseproof paper and make sure the bowl you'll whip your whites in is super-clean.

○ Tip in the egg whites and start whisking slowly until the whites start to foam, then, whether you're doing this manually or by machine, crank up the speed to medium–high.

○ Mix together the sugar and salt and add a tablespoon at a time, scraping down any detritus flung onto the side of the bowl with a spatula.

○ Once it's all in, go to max warp factor (full pelt) for 5 minutes until the mixture is super-firm and glossy.

○ Use two tablespoons to shape the meringues – one to scoop the mix and t'other to slide it onto the lined baking tray.

○ Put into the middle of the oven and straightaway turn the temperature down to 120°C/100°C fan/gas mark ½.

○ Bake for 1½ hours without opening the door at all, then turn the oven off – still no peeking – and leave to cool in the oven overnight.

SIMPLE TOFFEE SAUCE

100g caster sugar

100g cold butter, cut into squares

125ml double cream

○ Put the sugar and butter in a heavy-based saucepan on the smallest burner over a low–medium heat until the butter has melted.

○ Turn up the temperature a bit and keep stirring with a spatula pretty much all the time: the mix will bubble up and start to change colour from creamy to golden, and when you see it hit a lovely shade of fudge, take it off the heat immediately (and don't panic if it looks like it has split at this stage... the cream always seems to pull it together).

○ Grab a balloon whisk and whisk in the cream like billy-ho until it looks like a golden toffee sauce. NB: When the cream hits the hot fudge it will bubble up briefly; be careful not to get any on your skin as you whisk as it'll burn like the devil!

○ You need to get it down to room temp (not fridge-cold) to use for the mess, so if needed scrape it into a new vessel to chill out. I find there's no better place for cooling than the doorstep/window sill.

Timeline

NIGHT BEFORE

Cook meringues and leave in the oven (unopened) overnight

COUPLE OF HOURS BEFORE

Make the toffee sauce (so it's at room temp when you need it)

SOON BEFORE SERVING:

Toast almonds

Whip up Biscuity Chantilly

Slice nanas

Construction (hi-vis optional)

BISCUITY CHANTILLY

300ml double cream

2 tablespoons caster sugar

½ teaspoon vanilla extract

8 digestive biscuits, broken up into biggish pieces

○ Either in a mixer or in a big bowl with a balloon whisk, lightly whip the cream with the sugar – slow down as you see/feel it thicken.

○ Turn through the vanilla and broken biccy pieces.

THE BUILD
(AKA 'THE MESS')

GOOD FOR 10–12 KIDS OR 6–8 BIG KIDS (AKA GROWN-UPS)

20g flaked almonds

3 bananas

Sea Salt Meringues (see previous page)

Simple Toffee Sauce (see previous page) – not hard from the fridge; it needs to be at room temperature

Biscuity Chantilly (see above)

couple of squares of dark or milk chocolate, for grating

○ Preheat the oven to 180°C/ 160°C fan/gas mark 4. Spread the almonds out on a baking tray and pop them in the oven as it's warming up for 12ish minutes, giving them a bit of a shuffle around halfway through: the deeper side of golden is what you're looking for.

○ Peel and slice the nanas into chunky bite-sized pieces and roughly break the meringues in half.

○ Put them both in a large mixing bowl, splodge in half the toffee sauce, then fold in the Biscuity Chantilly cream in a way that doesn't break up the meringues too much.

○ Spoon onto anything flat that you're happy to serve on in a high pile, then grate on the choccy, throw on the toasted almonds and finish by zigzagging over the remainder of the toffee sauce (a squeezy bottle moment if ever there was one). Now stand back and admire your edifice of nurseryness before the mass dive into the mess.

dark & stormy gingerbread

DARK & STORMY GINGERBREAD

PREP: 20 MINS • COOK 1 HOUR • LEAVE: 10 DAYS

HOME-MADE WHIPPED LIME BUTTER
(YOU MAKE THE BUTTER!)

PREP: 15 MINS

ANGOSTURA HONEYCOMB

COOK • 10 MINS • LEAVE: TO COOL

When it comes to cocktails I'm not really a lover of long highballs: give me a hard and fast sidecar or anything in a martini glass that's basically wall-to-wall booze over a froufrou fruity fella any day.

But sometimes the temperature just calls for a tall guy, and on such an occasion I'll always ask for him to be Dark and Stormy.

The recipe for the super-sticky gingerbread at the heart of this knockout pud is based on a gift from the most talented pastry chef I know, Graham Hornigold (who doesn't just sound like it but truly is descended from a pirate). I was lucky enough to be his co-judge on CBBC's Junior Bake Off in 2015, and whilst I'm not sure how much the kids took away from it, for sure I tripled my patisserie knowledge in that kitschest of kitchen tents.

Of course you can choose not to make the butter from scratch, and just whip lime zest and icing sugar into half a pat of softened butter, but really it only takes a few minutes and when else are you going to make butter in your life?

And the last vital ingredient in a Dark and Stormy is, of course, those damn tasty psychedelic drops from Trinidad and Tobago. Angostura bitters are no less than 44.7 per cent alcohol, which is why they are famed as a hair of the dog, as well as for pink gin. I'm a firm believer that there's no such thing as an original idea in cookery – pretty much every base combo has been done before but differently to how you or I would, which is why cooking is quite so marvellous and utterly endless. Having said that, I'm pretty sure no one has ever put Angostura into honeycomb before...

You can eat these however you like, but I recommend slathering a slice of gingerbread with a thick layer of lime butter, then scattering over some shards of honeycomb for crunch and flavour.

P.S. The rum thing is entirely up for grabs: if there are kids to be fed, then I advocate cutting and wrapping the cooled cake in half, keeping the kiddy one as is, whilst feeding the grown-up's one the rum. My rum quantity, by the way, is just a guideline – the longer you leave it the more it happily absorbs... I have been known to get a quarter bottle in there over a full ten-day development session (the cake's, I mean, not mine).

DARK & STORMY GINGERBREAD

100g butter, plus extra for greasing

130g dark soft brown sugar

2½ tablespoons (70g) golden syrup

3 generous tablespoons (90g) black treacle

250g plain flour

1 heaped teaspoon ground ginger

1 teaspoon baking powder

¾ teaspoon bicarbonate of soda

good pinch of salt

40g preserved stem ginger, thinly sliced

1 egg

220ml milk

around 100+ml dark rum

○ Preheat the oven to 150°C/130°C fan/gas mark 2. Lightly grease a 22 x 13 x 6cm loaf tin with butter, then line with greaseproof paper.

○ Put the butter, sugar, golden syrup and treacle in a pan and warm together, but don't let the mix boil.

○ Sift the flour, ground ginger, baking powder, bicarb and salt into a mixing bowl, then stir in the stem ginger and make a well in the middle. Meanwhile, beat together the egg and milk, and set aside.

○ Stir the melted sugary liquids into the well, then using a wooden spoon, draw the flour in slowly; at first it will be a super-sticky batter, but then will bind together, form a ball and come away cleanly from the side of the bowl.

○ Swap your wooden spoon for a whisk and tip in the egg/milk mix in three stages, whisking till smooth between each batch.

○ Scrape into the prepared loaf tin and bake for about an hour until an inserted skewer comes out clean, then take out of the oven and leave to cool completely in the tin.

○ Use a skewer or thin knife to make 20–30 holes in the top of the cake reaching down to around the middle. Slowly pour in the rum until no more is visible on the top, then cover with clingfilm, tin and all.

○ Leave in a cool place for up to 10 days, feeding it with more rum if and when you feel like it: the flavour will keep developing for 4 days, then level out.

ANGOSTURA HONEYCOMB

plain oil; for greasing (like vegetable or sunflower)

150g golden caster sugar

75g golden syrup

2 tablespoons Angostura Bitters

2 teaspoons bicarbonate of soda

You'll find this easier with a sugar thermometer, but it's by no means essential.

○ Line a small roasting tray with greaseproof paper, lightly oil it with plain oil (belt and braces to stop it sticking) and put to one side.

○ Pour the sugar and golden syrup into a fair-sized heavy-based pan. Put over a medium heat and stick the sugar thermometer in there if you have one.

○ Nothing seems to be happening fast for a while, but my firm and sage advice is Do Not Attempt To Multitask Whilst Making Honeycomb. When it happens, it happens pretty quickly and dramatically, and if you're not on hand for that exact moment, then you'll be looking at a BIG caramel-cleaning nightmare. (NB: If you see crystals beginning to form on the sides of the pan, just dip a pastry brush into cold water and wipe the brush over the inside of the pan, taking care not to get the bristles in the caramel.)

○ Once it starts to turn from golden to reddish (around the 130°C mark), add the Angostura but do not stir – just swirl the pan to incorporate. Don't go anywhere while it goes a stage further to a dark amber hue (about 140°C), then quick as you can, whisk in the bicarb, turn off the heat and straightaway pour the foaming mass into the prepared tray.

○ Leave to cool completely, then crack or cut into geographic shards. (Useful to know it keeps fine in an airtight container overnight.)

HOME-MADE WHIPPED LIME BUTTER

MAKES A BIG RAMEKINFUL – ENOUGH FOR A HEALTHY SPREAD ON EACH SLICE OF GINGERBREAD

250ml double cream
4 tablespoons (40g) icing sugar
zest of 2 limes
pinch of salt

YOU MAKE THE BUTTER!

○ Put the cream in a stand mixer and start whisking slowly at first, then as it begins to thicken, increase the speed to high.

○ Watch with interest and awe as the cream goes through the soft peak stage, past stiff peaks, until it splits and looks a bit like scrambled eggs. Throughout this time, periodically stop the machine and scrape down the sides to keep everybody in the mix, as it were.

○ Keep spinning at high speed as the liquid separates from the solids; lay a cloth over the machine to stop it splashing around everywhere and making a mess.

○ Continue whisking on full whack for 5–7 minutes until all the liquid has come out and you are looking at a lump of butter sitting in a puddle of milkyness, aka buttermilk.

○ Set a sieve over a bowl and scrape the butter into it, keeping the buttermilk for pancakes (any Yank will tell you it's an essential ingredient).

○ Wash and dry the bowl from the mixer. Pat the top of the butter and the bottom of the sieve to remove surface moisture before tipping it back in, along with the icing sugar, lime zest and salt.

○ Whisk together for a literal minute until combined, then move into a small china bowl and either fridge it or keep at room temperature if the time is nigh.

Timeline

SOMEWHERE ROUNDABOUT A WEEK PRIOR

Make the gingerbread and start feeding it the booze

ON THE DAY/DAY BEFORE

Both the honeycomb and lime butter can happily sit overnight: just store the honeycomb in an airtight container and get your lime butter out of the fridge in time to soften.

However, if you're up for the craic/a bit short of time (and just to make you feel better, I'm generally both) you can bang through the pair of them in the hour before you serve. Little bit stressy though.

churros with dunkers & dippers

CHURRRRRRROS!!

PREP: 20 MINS · COOK 5-10 MINS

CINNAMON SUGAR

PREP: 2 MINS

PAY-PER-VIEW CHOCOLATE SAUCE

COOK: 5 MINS

The notion for this book is writ large on the cover: one dish that requires minimal input, just a shift from Old Father Time – and two lightning-quick bolt-ons.

But, I'll say it again, rules are there to be broken (a dictat I've never had any trouble with), and in this scenario not only is the star player here a fast one, but so are the supporting actors.

And actually if you really want to tear up the rule book and get the party started, spoil them silly with an extra couple of other dunkers 'n' dippers too: take a few minutes to knock up the Biscuity Chantilly (without the biscuits) and Simple Toffee Sauce (pages 195–6).

All of which would make this a Quick, Quick, Quick, Quick, Quick... sounds like a flock of posh ducks, non?

One of Delilah-daughter's All-time Star Puds.

Timeline

HALF AN HOUR BEFORE YOU'RE ABOUT TO MAKE A LOT OF FOLKS VERY HAPPY

Make the churros up to when the dough is cooling

Use the time to knock up the choc sauce and cinnamon sugar (and to any extra-milers out there, I'd do the toffee sauce before them and the chantilly cream after)

Then get your oil heating and once up to temp start piping churros... Happy daze!

 ## CHURRRRRRROS!!

MAKES ABOUT 24

200g plain flour

60g caster sugar, plus more for sprinkling

1 teaspoon salt

30g butter

1–1.5 litres plain frying oil (like vegetable or sunflower)

You will also need a piping bag fitted with a star nozzle (and you really do need a star nozzle or else they will just look like turds).

○ Weigh the flour and leave to the side. Put the sugar, salt and butter into a saucepan with 500ml water over a low heat, stirring regularly so that the butter melts and the sugar and salt dissolve.

○ Bring this to a simmer, not a boil, and then turn off immediately – you don't want the water to evaporate, as the water/steam is what makes the churros fluffy and light when frying.

○ Vigorously stir in the flour using a spatula or a wooden spoon. Keep beating for a couple of minutes until it becomes totally smooth, i.e. no flour bubbles, and starts to form into a ball that comes away from the side of the pan (a bit of a workout).

○ Leave to cool for 5ish minutes, and take this time to knock up the cinnamon sugar and easy-peasy chocolate sauce.

○ Now the fun starts: pour the oil into a high-sided saucepan and put over a high heat. It'll take a while (10ish mins) to come up to temp, so use this time to scrape the cooled churros mixture into a piping bag (I'd double bag if you're using disposables – this mix is pretty firm). Lay some kitchen paper on a tray, ready to receive and degrease your churros, and find yourself a pair of scissors.

○ There are two ways to tell if the oil is hot enough: the first and arguably easiest is that the temp hits 190°C on a sugar thermometer. The second also works fine: just drop a little ball of the batter in and if it sizzles and floats, then it's ready – make sure it doesn't overheat though as the churros will burn on the outside too quickly to cook the middle.

○ Squeeze the batter into the oil to a length of about 10–12cm, then snip it off with the scissors and carry on pushing out the next one; six at a time is plenty. Try not to land them on top of one another as they'll stick (although if they do, it's no biggie – just use scissors to snip them apart while they're cooking).

○ The churros should sizzle and start to float up; fry for 4–5 minutes until golden brown, turning regularly for even colouration. Use a slotted spoon to lift them onto the kitchen paper for a minute, then serve up straightaway with the cinnamon sugar and chockie sauce in little bowls while you get on with the next lot.

CINNAMON SUGAR

100g caster sugar

½ teaspoon ground cinnamon

○ Ta-da!

PAY-PER-VIEW CHOCOLATE SAUCE

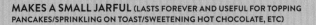

MAKES A JAM JARFUL

160ml double cream

½ teaspoon vanilla extract

100g chocolate (milk or dark or a mixture of both), cut into small pieces

AND IF IT'S FOR GROWN-UPS, ADD...

3 tablespoons pretty much anything sticky from the booze cupboard (Cointreau, Tia Maria, Kahlua, Drambuie, Grand Marnier... you get the idea)

around ¼ teaspoon cayenne pepper (depending on the size of your cahounas)

○ Put the cream and vanilla in a small pan and warm over a medium heat until steaming.

○ Tip in the chopped choccy and stir until smooth, adding the 18-certificate bits in now too if you're eligible (Terms and Conditions apply).

index

thanks & acknowledgements

QQS, as we call it, is not just my book but also belongs to a fine bunch of others, without whom it quite simply wouldn't have made it to fruition.

First up must be my culinary wing-woman on this job, Deniz Safa. She'd already supported me on my last book but rose to co-pilot on this one, from the conception of ideas to final delivery. Every single Saturday from October to March (with one off for Christmas, as every good Muslim needs) we cooked, laughed, cleared up and created. Nice going, and fun times too (none more so than watching you take a month to make and brew beer that then exploded all over my street). [and on that point a quick mention for both Mark Dredge (of www.pencilandspoon.com) and Mark Charlwood (of www.beerbirrabier.com) who both gave over-the-phone techy support to Deniz on the home-brew front but alas without making any difference to the outcome...though I'm still grateful for that priceless look on her face and our ensuing gut-aching, tear-streaming laughter as bottle after bottle exploded F1 style in her hands...well worth the two-month investment of time and money!].

Second up on the cooking front is my old buddy Dandan, who stepped in as 2nd lieutenant on the shoot. Always a pleasure, never a pain – even when we're both in it, and we're in it together babe.

And lastly to Guardian Angel Angelina, who had no official title or even reason to be helpful but just was, digging us out of the shit. When the prep list seemed impenetrable at 10 o'clock at night, you just walked in, got stuck in and Samurai'd your way through it.

In terms of the book itself, rather than kitchen graft, none of this would have been possible without the legend that is Kyle Cathie. This is my second book with Kyle, and somewhere between books one and two we have become friends as well as folks who work together, and my admiration and affection runs deep.

To Tara O'Sullivan, my editor: it has been a genuine pleasure getting this ship to sail with you. Your kindness, tenacity, understanding and desire for stress-free problem-solving means that you always keep everyone happy but never take your eyes off the prize. Nice work, sister.

Choosing the right designer can often be tricky, but the minute Anita Mangan's name was on the table it was a matter of job done. The way you reflect my words and recipes with weird and wonderful creative magic really does make the pages light up. Brava!

Words and design are all fine and dandy, but we all know that people really buy cookery books because of the photos, and I am proud and elated beyond belief with the shots in this book. Georgia Glynn-Smith (ably assisted by 'first to arrive and last to leave' Jen Rich) went beyond the call of duty to interpret my words into pictures and the results are there for all to see. Working with you again was nothing but a pleasure love. x

Big thanks too to Emily Ezekiel for all her propping, styling and generally standing up to this often bolshie chef!

It's important to me that the recipes in my books actually work, but not having the resource of a huge staff of recipe testers, time after time I have relied on my friends and family to come to my aid. What that actually means is that once I've got the recipes to a point at which I'm happy with them (anything from 2–15 cooks) I then send them out as word docs – no pics – to my nearest and dearest on the grounds that if they can cook them like that and get a result, I can breathe easy on setting them out in print. Their ingreds are unpaid, as is their time, and to be honest I have no idea why they sign up for it, but it remains to be said that I'm extremely grateful that they do.

And they are: Goddaughter Pillie (McTurco, thyme flatbread, beetroot tzatziki); Cousin Jen (Szechuan Belly, coleslaw, scoobie); Sister Floss (Tafelspitz, H'radish, Alpine tatties); head Honcho Hannah D (Crab laksa, sambal & shallots); boss 'n' buddy Claire (Brill, lovelies and anchovy aioli); Val 'The Frog' Laurent (Whiskey Salmon, Whiskey Brocc & Rice); Soup-sister Anita (Pork Burgers, bacon jam, quince aioli); Unflappable Alice (Bulgogi, noodles, explosion); Frances 'Still waters run deep' Crute (Pork shoulder, rosti, pie); Mega-Tosser Angelina (Ribs, sticky sauce, rice); NY-Lon Olly (Cheeky Bourguignon, smashed spuds, P & P); Isabelle GF (Prawn Linguine, preserved citrus, salmoriglio); Best ex-wife ever Susi (Duck curry, jasmine tea); Godmother Vicky (Red cabbage, Partridge, game chips); Friends since the 70s Juloo ... & Sadie-daughter (Party snarfes x 3); Best Beloveds in LA Marjan & Doug (Prune espresso torte etc); Fab Foodie Emily P (7:70, alpine spuds, freekeh); Godmother Loui ... & Gaia (Slow-cooked chook, pea dumplings, torn chix salad); Christina 'Max-mama' T (D & S gingerbread, lime butter, honeycomb); ole roomie James 'D&T' Nicholls (Bang-a-gong, bacon breadcrumbs, soup & muffs); Ninja James (Mutton madras, roti, raita); Super PA Rachel H (Calvados SF, poached fruit, French toast); Linda 'Fab' Fox (Banoffee mess); Big Sis Binky (Hake, Gk, EVOO spuds); BMF Justine (Ceviche, tostadas, aji verde); Caz 'bring on the bubbly' E (Summer rolls, do chua, Sriracha sce); new Osterlich buddy Sigrid... & Maebel (Churros, PPV choc sce, cinn sug); Special Agent Rosemary S (Poached chix, puffs, get better soup); Here in spirit Kate McC (Pork Ragu, Kale salad, pangrattata); Deniz's Super-sub Petra (Mussels, beer bread & vie frites AND Lamb Malplaquets, tabouleh, pom mol relish, bubble & baa)...& her BF David (Pilaff, Lebo salad, tzatsiki); Chaz The Charmer (3 x Obos); Stuart c/o Eames Consultancy (Rib-I, fondants, burnt butter Holl); Ladies with Roots: Ali J & Polly A (Jamaican Oxtail, festivals & plantains); Bolton's Best: Ali's Mum & Dad (Turkish beans, thyme flatbread, banging egg brekkie); BFF Sara (Agrodolce toms, sardines, salad); 'Sharp as a Sabatier' Belinda A (Lamb chops, pesto & WB salad); Enthusiastic Newcomer Hanna Barber (Squid, Szechuan aioli, blackened broccc); Aoife the Unshakeable (Scallops, do chua, bahn mi); Caring yet critical Catherine F (Paneer, sag, roti); 'More than just a Veggie' Philippa F (Baked butternut, pear salad, blue cheese dip).

And lastly on the cook front to Usha Gurnani, a friendly but firm pair of hands when my first shot at paneer was anything but.

My heartfelt thanks to each and every one of you xxx

Everyone knows that you can't make good food without good ingredients, but I'd go as far as saying that to me it's just as important where and who I get my goods from. The following people not only supply me with the best, freshest and most pleasing to cook ingredients, but also are unswervingly there to answer my questions and queries in their specialist fields...and with a welcome bit of chat and banter too:

Rodney, Damien and all at Macken Brothers (mackenbros.co.uk)

Tony, Jerome and the team at The Fishmongers Kitchen (fishmongerskitchen.com)

Veronica, Des and everyone at DPP (ddpltd.org)

In terms of personal support, my life would simply not be as I know it without my agent Rosemary Scoular at United Agents. More than just a sounding board, Rosemary is always there when I need her and after so many years it's fair to say that I now value our friendship more than our professional relationship.

Behind every great woman there's another great woman, and in Rosemary's case it's the friendly force that is Aoife Rice: I'm so eternally grateful for all the time and trouble you take to iron out the wrinkles in my life.

And lastly to the home front: for reasons of existing work commitments and to some degree failure on my part to realise the enormity of the task of thinking about, cooking and writing this book, there are a few folks who stepped in/up to look after Delilah-daughter when I was stuck at the stove/keyboard. Big love and thanks to Justine, Thess, Caz and Catherine S-K for doing the most important job when I just couldn't.

And lastly to my family: to someday-ex-mother-in-law Sarah – thank you for the quiet of your flat as well as your unerring support; to Susi for being the best nearly-ex-wife ever; and Isabelle for bearing with me, giving me strength and above all making life the adventure it should be.

& D. Just because you are.